SPORTS HEROES AND LEGENDS ™

Tiger Woods

Read all of the books in this exciting,
action-packed biography series!

Hank Aaron

Barry Bonds

Joe DiMaggio

Tim Duncan

Dale Earnhardt Jr.

Lou Gehrig

Derek Jeter

Michelle Kwan

Mickey Mantle

Jesse Owens

Ichiro Suzuki

Tiger Woods

SPORTS HEROES AND LEGENDS™

Tiger Woods

by Matt Doeden

Lerner Publications Company/Minneapolis

For Gina, my own golfing partner

Copyright © 2005 by Lerner Publications Company

Sports Heroes and Legends™ is a trademark of Barnes and Noble.

Used with permission from Barnes and Noble.

Lerner Publications Company
A division of Lerner Publishing Group
241 First Avenue North
Minneapolis, MN 55401 U.S.A.

Website address: www.lernerbooks.com

Cover photograph:
© SportsChrome East/West, Michael Zito

Library of Congress Cataloging-in-Publication Data

Doeden, Matt.
    Tiger Woods / by Matt Doeden.
        p.   cm. — (Sports heroes and legends)
    Includes bibliographical references and index.
    ISBN-13: 978–0–8225–3082–4 (lib. bdg. : alk. paper)
    ISBN-10: 0–8225–3082–1 (lib. bdg. : alk. paper)
    1. Woods, Tiger—Juvenile literature. 2. Golfers—United States—
Biography—Juvenile literature. I. Title. II. Series.
GV964.W66D64 2005
796.352'092—dc22   2004028564

Manufactured in the United States of America
1 2 3 4 5 6 – JR – 10 09 08 07 06 05

Contents

Prologue

Young Master

Twenty-one-year-old Tiger Woods stepped onto the green at the final hole of the 1997 Masters Tournament, golf's greatest event. He had been a professional golfer for less than a year, but his sweet swing and signature red shirt had already made him the most famous golfer in the world.

A huge crowd gathered around the green, eager to watch the young star sink his putt and become the youngest Masters champion. Tiger had dreamed of this moment all his life.

The event began on Thursday, April 10, in Augusta, Georgia. Tiger had been nervous at first, and he didn't play well. On the first nine holes, he'd shot a score of 40, four strokes over par. It wasn't good enough, and he knew it. (Par for the course was 72.) "I was bringing the club almost parallel to the ground on my backswing," he said. "That was way too long for me. I knew I had to shorten the swing."

Tiger made the adjustment on his swing and went on to shoot six under par for the last nine holes of the day. He finished with a score of 70, two strokes under par. Friday was even better. Tiger shot a 66, six strokes under par, and took the lead. On Saturday, he had one of the best rounds in the history of the Masters, shooting a 65 and building a huge lead over the other golfers in the field.

Everyone in the golf world knew that Tiger had talent, but very few expected the young player to dominate golf's biggest event as he had. For a few days, Tiger was about as close to perfect as a golfer can be. He hit the fairway on almost every drive. Nearly every approach shot put him in good putting position. And almost every putt found a line to the hole.

"I've never played an entire tournament with my A-game," Tiger later said. "This is pretty close—sixty-three holes. Excluding [the front nine], I pretty much had my A-game the whole week."

When he stepped onto the course on Sunday, the final day of the tournament, Tiger held a commanding nine-stroke lead. But the pressure wasn't off. Tiger's amazing week had put him in position to set the record for the best overall score in Masters history. A Sunday score of 70 would give him 271 overall, which would tie the record held by Jack Nicklaus and Ray Floyd.

Tiger teed off on the 18th hole with a score of 65. He needed only to par the hole to finish with a score of 270, which would beat the record. His tee shot turned left, though, and missed the fairway. But the bad shot didn't affect Tiger. He recovered and gave himself a short putt attempt for par. The crowd grew quiet as he lined up the putt that would seal his place in golf history. As the ball dropped into the cup, the crowd roared. Tiger pumped his fist in the air. He walked toward his parents. Tiger closed his eyes and hugged his father. He was the youngest Masters champion in history, with the best score in history.

Tiger had shot eighteen under par for the tournament, beating second-place Tom Kite by twelve strokes. He was on his way to becoming the greatest golfer in the world.

Chapter One

Birth of a Tiger

Eldrick "Tiger" Woods was born on December 30, 1975. His father, Earl, had been a U.S. Army Green Beret and fought in the Vietnam War (1959–1975). During the war, Earl spent some time in Thailand. There he met a woman named Kultida, known as Tida, who worked as a secretary in a U.S. Army office. The two quickly fell in love. When Earl's war service was complete, he brought Tida back to the United States with him. They married in 1969. It was Earl's second marriage.

Six years later, Tida gave birth to Eldrick. It was a name she made up, using the first letter of Earl's name for the beginning

 Tiger has two half brothers and one half sister from his father's first marriage.

4

and the first letter of her name for the end. Earl agreed to the name, but he knew that he would always call his son "Tiger."

During the war, Earl had fought alongside a South Vietnamese soldier named Vuong Dang Phong. The two soldiers became great friends, and Phong saved Earl's life several times. Earl thought Phong was strong and brave, and he gave his friend the nickname "Tiger." Phong disappeared during the war, and Earl didn't know what had happened to him. But he vowed to call his son Tiger in Phong's honor.

"I hoped my son would be as courageous as my friend," Earl explained. "I also hoped that someday, somehow, Phong would see the names Tiger and Woods together and make the connection." Earl's reunion with his friend never happened, though. Years later he learned that Phong had died shortly after the war ended.

Around the time Tiger was born, Earl became very interested in golf. Earl had been a baseball player in college, and when a friend taught him to golf, he became fascinated by the sport. Earl was talented, but he knew he had started too late in life to ever be a great golfer. As he looked at his infant son, he dreamed that one day Tiger could show the world that a black man could be a star in a sport that was dominated by white athletes.

Earl built himself a practice driving range in the garage. He set up a net to catch the balls that he drove off of a small piece of carpet. Earl spent hours in his driving range, with Tiger often sitting in his high chair, watching. Tiger was still too young to walk or talk, but watching his father hit golf balls was already one of his favorite activities.

GOLF TERMS

Par—the number of strokes a good golfer should expect
  to need on a hole
Birdie—one stroke less than par
Eagle—two strokes less than par
Bogey—one stroke more than par
Front nine—the first nine holes of a round
Back nine—the last nine holes of a round
Fairway—the short-cut grass between the tee
  and the green
Green—the very short-cut grass that surrounds a hole

When Tiger was nine months old, Earl cut down a club for him to swing. Tiger held the club and stood in front of the ball. Earl was shocked to see the child bring the club back and make a good swing. On his first try, Tiger hit the ball into the net. Earl knew right away that his son had a gift.

Little Tiger loved to golf. His mother gave him a tennis ball and the end of a vacuum hose. Tiger would hit the ball around the house, practicing his swing and ignoring his other toys. Earl brought Tiger to visit his first driving range at a real golf course when he was just eighteen months old. Soon after, he played his first hole of golf, a long par four. Tiger sank his putt on his eleventh stroke.

As Tiger grew, his game improved. By age four, he regularly played at a short par-three course called Heartwell Golf Park. Rudy Duran, an assistant pro at the course, watched Tiger. Duran, like other course professionals and assistant pros, was an expert golfer who worked at the course and helped people improve their games. He was amazed at how well the child could play, and he agreed to become Tiger's first teacher.

Tiger still didn't have the strength to make par on most holes. Duran worried that the youngster might lose confidence if he kept shooting over par all the time. So Duran invented a new

---

YOUNG CELEBRITY

When Tiger was two, he was invited to appear on *The Mike Douglas Show*. On the show, comedian Bob Hope challenged Tiger to a putting contest. Tiger missed three putts and became angry. He threw the ball into the cup and told Douglas that the green wasn't level. Three years later, Tiger appeared on the television show *That's Incredible!*, where he hit Wiffle balls into the crowd.

"Tiger par" for each hole. Tiger par was the score that Duran felt Tiger should be able to get on each hole.

While Earl worked with Tiger and his golf game, Tida made sure that Tiger took school seriously. Tiger was a good student and got along with most of his classmates. But he lived in a neighborhood with mostly white people. On his first day of kindergarten, several white students tied him to a tree and called him racist names. Tiger was very upset, even after the students were caught and punished. But Earl told him that he had to learn to ignore people who called him names. Earl knew Tiger would struggle against racism in his life no matter what he did, but it would be even worse if he became a golfer. Tiger had to learn that what others said couldn't affect him.

Despite the distractions, Tiger continued to excel in school and in golf. Tida wouldn't let Tiger play golf until he had finished his homework. She told Tiger that he couldn't be sure that he would be able to make a living as a professional golfer. He had to have a good education, just in case. One of Tiger's teachers suggested that he skip a grade, but he refused. He wanted to stay with children his own age. But while Tiger chose not to pass his fellow students at school, he was passing golfers twice his age on the course.

When Tiger was six, he played a match against Stewart Reed, a professional golfer. Tiger actually held a lead early in the match, but Reed went on to win. Tiger was so angry that he wouldn't shake Reed's hand. Tida scolded her son and told him that he couldn't behave that way. He had to learn to be a good sport, even when he lost.

Later, Tiger got to play another professional, Sam Snead, a golf legend from the 1940s and 1950s. They played the final two holes at Soboba Springs Country Club in southern California. Tiger's first shot sailed right. But he recovered and scored a 4, one over par. Snead beat Tiger by only one stroke. Snead was impressed by the way Tiger played, but he was even more impressed by how he acted. When Snead offered young Tiger his autograph, Tiger grinned and offered Snead his autograph.

___

66*I was blown away. It was unbelievable. [Tiger] was awesome. . . . I felt like he was Mozart. He was like a shrunken touring pro. . . . It was genius.*99

—RUDY DURAN

___

Tiger was still six when he played his first real tournament. He entered the ten-and-under division of the Optimist Junior World Championship. Tiger finished eighth out of 150 golfers. The seven boys who beat him were all ten years old.

When Tiger was eight, he won his age division at the Junior World Championship. He shot an amazing five under par at the

9

short Presidio Hills Golf Course in San Diego, California. He won the event again the next year. By the time he was ten, he was ready to compete in the division for eleven- and twelve-year-olds. Two years later, he won again.

Tiger's golf game wasn't the only thing in his life. He continued to do well in school. Tida also took him to Thailand to teach him about his roots there. She brought him to see a Buddhist monk. Tida follows the Buddhist religion, and she wanted Tiger to learn more about it. The monk said that he could tell Tiger was special and that one day he would become a leader.

Many people think of Tiger as an African American, but he actually has a much more complex ethnic heritage. His father is only half African American. He's also a quarter American Indian and a quarter Chinese. His mother is half Thai, a quarter Chinese, and a quarter white.

In 1986, when Tiger was ten, the magazine *Golf Digest* published a story about legendary golfer Jack Nicklaus. The story included a list of his major achievements and the age at which he'd achieved them. Tiger cut the list out of the magazine and kept it. Most people considered Nicklaus the greatest golfer ever. Tiger wanted to be better. To do that, he wanted to do everything

Nicklaus had done in golf, and he wanted to do it at a younger age.

Tiger often imagined himself playing against great golfers of the time, like Greg Norman and Tom Watson. He imagined what kinds of shots he would need to make to beat the best golfers in the world.

When Tiger was thirteen, he played an event called the Insurance Youth Golf Classic, or "Big I." On the final day, professional golfers joined the youngsters for a round. Tiger was paired with John Daly, a professional famous for his long drives. Tiger took an early lead in the round, and Daly joked that he hoped a kid wasn't going to beat him. But Tiger continued to play well, and he led Daly by two strokes after the first nine holes. Daly stepped his game up on the back nine with four birdies and held on to beat Tiger.

 Tiger scored his first hole in one when he was only eight years old.

"That kid is great," Daly said. "Everybody was applauding him and nobody applauded me. He's better than I'd heard."

Tiger's fame continued to grow. People began talking about his future as a professional golfer. Tiger even received a letter from Wally Goodwin, the golf coach at Stanford University. Tiger thought about Stanford frequently. His education was still important to his mother, and golf was important to Tiger and his father. Stanford was one of the finest universities in the country, and it had an excellent golf team. It seemed like a perfect fit. Tiger was only in seventh grade, but he was already making decisions that would shape his future.

Chapter Two

Dominating the Juniors

Tiger was growing quickly, both physically and in his ability on the golf course. But Earl still worried about Tiger's mental game. Tiger was a teenager, so Earl decided it was time to be tougher on him.

Earl would often go to a course or a driving range with his son and make small golf bets. They would have driving contests, each hitting a ball as far as he could. Whoever had the longer drive won. Tiger could easily outdrive his father, so Earl added a twist to the bets. The drive had to land on the fairway. If Tiger's ball rolled even an inch off the fairway, Earl won.

Earl also worked to break Tiger's concentration at key moments. During practice, he would often cough loudly just as Tiger was beginning his swing. Other times, when Tiger was putting, Earl would stand so his shadow fell over the hole, making it difficult to see. Earl hoped all of these actions would help

Tiger deal with difficult situations later in life. "I was determined that he'd never run up against someone mentally stronger than he was," Earl said.

Tiger also listened to cassette tapes with subliminal messages, positive phrases hidden behind other sounds. People can't hear subliminal messages with their conscious minds, but many believe that the subconscious mind understands them. Earl thought the messages would help Tiger's confidence and mental toughness.

TRAINING A TIGER

Earl Woods wrote a book, *Training a Tiger,* about how he raised Tiger to be a champion. Woods described how he used his love for Tiger and his passion for golf to teach Tiger to be the best golfer he could be.

Finally, Earl asked a psychologist to help Tiger. Jay Brunza was a psychologist for the U.S. Naval Academy. He worked with Tiger to improve his concentration and attention to detail. "[Tiger] doesn't need motivation from anybody else," Brunza said. "His motivation comes from within. I don't see him ever burning out, because golf is pure pleasure for him."

Tiger knew that mental strength alone wasn't enough to make a champion. He needed a strong body as well. He read about an exercise program that was supposed to help golfers and immediately started doing the suggested exercises. By age fifteen, Tiger had grown to almost six feet tall. He was very thin, but the exercises kept him strong. Tiger joined the golf team at Western High in Anaheim, California. Even as a freshman, Tiger was the top golfer on the team.

> 66 *That little whippersnapper was driving it by me. . . . Not only is his game solid but his all-around presence with questions and ambiance is fabulous. I'm just impressed by the guy.* 99
> —GREG NORMAN, AFTER PLAYING AGAINST TIGER IN 1991

All of Tiger's hard work on and off the golf course paid off. He was already the best junior amateur golfer in the country. But he set his sights much higher. In 1991 he decided that he wanted to qualify for a professional event, the Los Angeles Open. If he could make the field, he'd be the youngest golfer ever to take part in a PGA Tour event. The PGA Tour is the highest level of golf, featuring the world's top players. Because he was an amateur, Tiger couldn't make money for playing in the tournament. But he could still test his skills against professional golfers.

Tiger and 131 other players gathered on the South Course at Los Serranos Golf Course in Chino Hills, California. All of the players were competing for two open spots in the tournament. Many of Tiger's opponents were more than twice his age.

Tiger had a fast start in his qualifying round. He made birdies on the fifth and sixth holes. Then on the seventh hole, he made a shot from forty yards out for an eagle. Tiger continued to shoot well, and by the time he reached the last hole, he needed to make another eagle to get into the tournament. Tiger's drive left him in a tough spot, and his second shot went into the water. Most of the other golfers were amazed at how close Tiger had come to qualifying for the tournament. But Tiger, who wasn't used to failure, was disappointed.

"You try to avoid envy in golf, but that kid humbled all of us," said Ron Hinds, one of Tiger's playing partners that day. "I felt myself rooting for him. I was hoping he'd get into the tournament so I could watch this awesome kid play against [Tom] Kite and [Ben] Crenshaw and those guys."

Tiger entered the 1991 U.S. Junior Amateur, held at Bay Hill Club in Orlando, Florida. The Junior Amateur is the top tournament for junior golfers (golfers younger than nineteen). Tiger advanced to the final match against Brad Zwetschke. If Tiger could win, he would become the youngest player ever to win the event.

GOLF SCORING

The goal of golf is to get the lowest score possible. Every swing counts as one stroke, whether it's a 300-foot drive or a two-foot putt. Each hole has a set par, which is the total number of strokes a good golfer should expect to take to finish the hole. Par for almost all golf holes is three, four, or five. A golfer who finishes under par for a hole takes fewer strokes than is expected. A golfer who finishes over par takes more strokes.

Tiger fell behind early in the match. He was down three shots after just six holes. But he came back and took the lead going into the final hole. With a chance to win, he drove the ball out of bounds and allowed Zwetschke to send the match to a playoff.

The bad shot could have shaken the young golfer, but Tiger didn't let it get to him. "I forgot about what I did on eighteen and worried about my tee shot," he explained. "I try to think one shot at a time."

Tiger quickly made up for his mistake by shooting par on the first playoff hole. Zwetschke missed a short par putt, and Tiger was the winner. Soon after his victory, the magazine

Golf Digest named Tiger the top junior player in the entire country.

As Tiger's fame grew, so did the pressure to succeed. Some people started calling him the great African American hope, the first real chance for an African American to change the world of golf. Tiger was honored to have his name mentioned with other African American golfers, such as Lee Elder, Charlie Sifford, and Calvin Peete, but he didn't like comparing himself to them.

"I don't want to be the best *black* golfer on the Tour," he said. "I want to be the best *golfer* on the Tour, period."

Late in 1991, an official from the Los Angeles Open invited Tiger to play in the event, which took place in February 1992. The official offered Tiger a sponsor's invitation, which meant Tiger didn't have to qualify for the tournament like other golfers. He'd play as an amateur, so he wouldn't be paid. (If he accepted any money for play during high school, he wouldn't be eligible for a college golf scholarship.)

Large crowds gathered to watch the young golfer who was quickly becoming the talk of the golf world. Tiger didn't disappoint the fans on his first professional hole, making a birdie on a long par five. But as the day went on, he missed several shots and finished with a score of 72, one over par.

Tiger was disappointed with his play. He knew he would need to play well the second day to make the cut. After the first two days of a professional tournament, only the top golfers get to continue. Those who score below the cut are out of the competition. Tiger was determined to make the cut, but his second day was worse than his first. He shot a 75, four over par, and missed the cut by six shots. Tiger was out of his first professional tournament, but just three days later, he helped his high school team to a tournament win.

As a teenager, Tiger often helped at clinics teaching young players to golf. He and Earl put on demonstrations. Sometimes Earl would stand about ten feet in front of his son while Tiger took shots over his head.

Although he was used to success, Tiger also suffered some setbacks during his time at Western High. In tenth grade, Tiger led the school's golf team to the league championship. On the last hole, Tiger's ball was on the green. He needed only to make the hole in two putts to clinch the win for his team. His first shot, a long putt, sailed past the hole. The second putt, for the win, narrowly missed the hole, resting only several inches away. He had blown his chance to clinch the victory for Western High.

Tiger walked up to his ball, needing only to tap it in for a tie. But instead of taking his time and doing it right, Tiger quickly tapped the ball, eager to get the hole over with. His lack of concentration cost him. The ball hit the edge of the hole but didn't go in. Western High lost the championship, and Tiger blamed himself.

Tiger's life was growing increasingly busy. Because he had won the Junior Amateur, Tiger had earned a chance to play in the U.S. Amateur and to qualify for the 1992 U.S. Open. He made a solid attempt in the U.S. Amateur but did not advance to match play. Next came his chance to qualify for the U.S. Open. The U.S. Open is one of the four top tournaments in professional golf. But in the week before the qualifying round, he had final exams at school, and the day after the round, he had to take his driver's test. Tiger had to go to school, come home, study, and practice. He hardly had time to sleep. When the qualifying day finally came, Tiger didn't have his best game. His driving was good, but he struggled with his putting and didn't qualify.

Tiger didn't feel too bad about missing the U.S. Open. His attention was on the U.S. Junior Amateur that summer. Nobody had ever won the tournament twice, and Tiger intended to be the first.

The first part of the Junior Amateur is like a regular tournament. All of the players compete against one another for the lowest scores. This is called stroke play. Tiger easily won the stroke play part of the tournament. The second part is a match play tournament. In match play, two golfers match up and play against each other. Instead of counting total strokes, each hole is a separate contest. Golfers count the number of holes each player wins. Matches don't always go a full eighteen holes. The match ends as soon as one golfer can't catch the other.

Tiger dominated his early opponents in match play. He beat one of them by a score of 8 and 6, which means Tiger beat the other golfer by eight holes, and the match was stopped with six holes left.

In the final round, Tiger played Mark Wilson for the championship. Wilson was tougher competition for Tiger. The match was tied going into the final hole, but Tiger's tap-in for bogey won him the tournament. Tiger cried as he celebrated. He had accomplished one of his goals—to become the first player to win two Junior Amateur titles.

Tiger's win earned him the chance to play in the U.S. Amateur. There Tiger had a terrible first round, hitting balls into the water, missing short putts, and losing his temper. He wasn't happy with his score of 78. He recovered in the second round, though, playing a nearly perfect round for a score of 66. His great second round helped him make the cut and advance to the match play part of the tournament. Tiger won his first match but lost in the second round to a college player named Tim Herron.

Tiger returned home, where he continued to dominate junior events. He began to grow bored of the competition at that level,

BUTCH HARMON

In August 1993, young Tiger was struggling with his swing at the U.S. Amateur Championship in Houston, Texas. Earl Woods decided his son needed help. A local coach in Houston, Butch Harmon, had gained some fame for helping Greg Norman win the British Open that year. Earl called Harmon and asked him to take a look at Tiger's swing. Harmon was impressed right away. The three all agreed that Harmon should take over for Earl as Tiger's coach.

Harmon is the son of Claude Harmon, the 1948 Masters champion. He played on the PGA Tour from 1969 to 1971, but he soon realized that he enjoyed teaching more than playing.

but he had one more goal before he left the junior ranks behind. He wanted to win a third straight Junior Amateur title. It was his only goal for the summer before his senior year.

Tiger started off well and he easily made the match play round, then won his way into the final match against Ryan Armour. Armour was tough. After sixteen holes, Armour led by 2. Tiger had to win both the 17th and 18th holes just to send the match into a playoff. If he lost either hole, it would be over.

Tiger made a birdie on the 17th and won the hole. He and Armour walked to the par-five 18th. Tiger appeared to be in deep trouble when his second shot went into a bunker, leaving him a difficult shot to the green. Tiger's approach shot was especially tricky because he was coming at the green from a tough angle. He was aiming at a very small area, and controlling his ball would be difficult from the sand. But he stroked a nearly perfect shot that rolled to about eight feet from the pin. He made his birdie putt and won the hole. He then went on to beat Armour in the playoff.

Tiger had won his third straight Junior Amateur. He knew there was nothing left for him to achieve in the junior ranks.

Chapter | Three

Eyes on the U.S. Amateur

During his last year of high school, Tiger officially decided to attend Stanford. Other universities had tried to change his mind, but he had known for years that Stanford would be his choice. It was a perfect mix of academics and athletics.

66He's probably one of the first players who doesn't have to go to college. He could turn pro immediately. He's going to be great.99

—JOHN DALY

Tiger graduated from high school with honors in 1994. That summer, his mind wasn't just on his future life at Stanford. Tiger's first concern was the U.S. Amateur in Ponte Vedra Beach, Florida. His days of playing juniors events were behind him, and he was ready to start competing with golfers much older and more experienced than he was. A wide range of players take part in the U.S. Amateur. Many, like Tiger, are young golfers who are preparing for a professional career. Others are older golfers who are very good but either can't or don't want to pursue a professional career.

Before Tiger competed in the U.S. Amateur, he had a few warm-up tournaments at that level. He started with the Pacific Northwest Amateur in Vancouver, Washington. Tiger played brilliantly. He made the final match, where he faced Oregon's amateur champion, Ted Snavely, in a thirty-six-hole match.

Tiger said before the match that he believed he would have a good round. Snavely played well, but he was hopelessly outclassed. Tiger played nearly perfectly. His drives carried long and straight, his approach shots found the green, and his putts held perfect lines to the hole. Tiger needed to play only twenty-six of the scheduled thirty-six holes to defeat Snavely 11 and 10. In those twenty-six holes, he shot an amazing thirteen under par. Tiger had proved that stepping up out of the junior class had been the right thing to do. "He played some fantastic golf, better than anyone else has played around here," said golf pro Steve Bowen.

Tiger built on his success by easily winning his next amateur event, the Southern California Golf Association Amateur. He had one event left to play, the Western Amateur, before the U.S. Amateur.

After making the cut in stroke play, Tiger advanced to match play. He won his first match and met Chris Tidland in the quarterfinals. Tiger held a big lead early, but Tidland came back to send the match into a playoff. Tidland put the pressure on Tiger in the first hole of the playoff, making a birdie, but Tiger came back with an eagle to win the match. Tiger went on to win the event, making him three for three in amateur events.

The U.S. Amateur—the moment Tiger had been waiting for—came in August 1994. Tiger confidently stepped onto the Sawgrass Stadium Course at the Tournament Players Club in Ponte Vedra Beach, Florida. He knew he was playing better than he ever had in his life.

A NARROW MISS

Tiger almost missed out on the 1994 U.S. Amateur. The day before the qualifying round, heavy traffic on the way to the airport caused Tiger and Earl to miss their flight. All the later flights were sold out. Father and son had to wait on standby, hoping seats would open up. They finally caught a very late flight, and Tiger arrived at the course in time.

Everything started smoothly for eighteen-year-old Tiger. He easily made the cut after stroke play. In his first match, he scored a close 2 and 1 win over forty-six-year-old Vaughn

Moise. Tiger's second match was even better—he scored an easy 6 and 5 victory over Michael Flynn.

Tiger advanced to the third round and an interesting opponent, Buddy Alexander. Alexander was a former U.S. Amateur champion, and he was from nearby Jacksonville. The crowds cheered hard for their local golfer. Many in the crowd thought they could rattle young Tiger, and they may have succeeded early on. Tiger quickly fell behind, trailing by four after the first eight holes.

Alexander began missing shots on the back nine, and Tiger saw an opening. He attacked, hitting several long, straight drives and making his putts. With two holes left, the match was all square, or tied.

On the 17th hole, Tiger almost had a golfing disaster. A pond lies to the left of the fairway, and Tiger's tee shot sailed toward it. The ball bounced, then came to rest only two feet from the water, giving him a chance to recover and save par. Alexander shot a bogey, and Tiger took the lead.

"I nearly passed out," Tiger later said when asked about the dangerous shot. He had needed a little luck, and he had gotten it.

Tiger almost gave the lead back on the final hole. He hit his tee shot out of bounds, but Alexander sent his shot into the water. Tiger held on and advanced to the quarterfinals, where he scored a 5 and 4 win over Tim Jackson.

Tiger won his next match, against Eric Frishette, to advance to the final. As with the U.S. Junior Amateur, the final match of the U.S. Amateur takes place over thirty-six holes.

In the final, Tiger's opponent was Trip Kuehne, whom Tiger considered a friend. But Tiger wasn't about to let up just because he was playing against a friend. As the final match started, however, Tiger quickly saw that he wasn't the hottest golfer on the course. Kuehne made birdies on seven of the first thirteen holes, while Tiger struggled. Suddenly Tiger found himself six down. It was a huge deficit. Nobody had ever come back to win the event after being down that many holes.

GOLF CLUBS

Golf clubs fall into one of three categories: woods, irons, and putters. Woods are long and have large club heads. Golfers get their longest shots with woods (the longest-hitting wood is called a driver). Irons are shorter clubs with narrow, angled club faces. The higher the number of an iron, the greater the angle of the club face. For example, a three iron has a mostly flat face, while a nine iron has a more horizontal angle. The more angle an iron has, the higher the shot goes. Sand wedges and other wedges are types of irons. Putters are flat. They work only for short, rolling shots.

After a lunch break, Earl took Tiger aside. He said, "Son, let the legend grow."

For a while, it didn't look like Tiger was going to mount a comeback. With twelve holes remaining, he was still five down. Kuehne was playing well, and it would be tough to make up that many holes against a good golfer.

One hole at a time, Tiger worked at the comeback. With nine holes left, he had cut Kuehne's lead to three. After Tiger made par on the tenth hole and a birdie on the 11th, the lead was cut to one.

The golfers tied the next several holes. When they walked to the tee at sixteen, the lead was still one. Tiger's tee shot missed the fairway, but he made a nice save and hit his birdie putt to tie the match. Only two more holes separated him from achieving one of his biggest goals.

Tiger paid close attention as he prepared to hit his shot off the 17th tee. From this spot, he had nearly put his shot into the water in his match with Alexander. Tiger held a nine iron in his hands as he looked toward the pin. Using the nine iron to put the ball on the middle green was the safe shot. But Tiger didn't want to go with the safe shot. A safe shot, he thought, was for a lesser player. Instead he grabbed his pitching wedge, a club that doesn't hit the ball as far. With water all around, it was a dangerous club selection. But Tiger had the wind at his back and he felt strong. "The pin," he later said. "I was going directly at the pin."

Tiger settled himself, pulled back the club, and ripped a perfect swing. The ball sailed high in the air, finally landing on the green only a few feet from the water's edge. The ball bounced toward the rough, then spun back onto the green, stopping only three feet from the water and fourteen feet from the hole. Tiger sank his putt and completed the comeback. He pumped his fist in celebration.

Tida watched the dangerous shot from home. "That boy almost gave me a heart attack," she said. "All I kept saying was, 'God, don't let that ball go in the water.' That boy tried to kill me."

LETTER FROM THE PRESIDENT

After his 1994 U.S. Amateur title, Tiger received a letter from President Bill Clinton. The letter included the following passage: "I commend you for the sportsmanship, discipline, and perseverance that earned you this great honor. Best wishes for every success at Stanford."

When Kuehne missed a short putt on the 18th hole, he conceded, or gave up, the match to Tiger. The two golfers and friends shook hands and hugged. Tiger then hugged his father as the crowd cheered the youngest champion in the history of the U.S. Amateur.

Until that point, Tiger had been well known only among people who paid close attention to golf. But this win attracted the attention of people who didn't typically follow the sport. Talk show hosts Jay Leno and David Letterman wanted him on their programs. His hometown of Cypress, California, gave him the key to the city to honor him. Newspapers put Tiger's picture on the front page. Even U.S. president Bill Clinton sent him a letter of congratulations. In only a few months, Tiger had taken over the world of amateur golf.

Chapter Four

Stanford Cardinal

Tiger enjoyed his record-setting win in the U.S. Amateur, but he was also excited about the next step in his life. He was headed to Stanford, where new academic and athletic challenges awaited him.

Life at Stanford was different. Tiger was on his own, without his parents constantly looking after him. But he knew what he wanted out of school. He made friends and played golf, but he also studied hard, majoring in economics. He wanted to make the most of his college years. Life as a professional golfer wouldn't be easy. Tiger wanted to enjoy this time with other young people.

Tiger and his teammates got along well. They spent hours at the driving range, hitting balls as far as they could. Nobody could crush the ball like Tiger. His teammates often sat around just watching him drive ball after ball.

The golf team treated Tiger like any other freshman on the team. They played practical jokes on him. They made him carry their luggage on trips. They made him sleep on the worst bed in hotel rooms. They even made up nicknames for their new star. They called him "Urkel" because he reminded them of a character from the television show *Family Matters.* They even laughed at him for his bad dancing. Tiger didn't mind the teasing too much. He enjoyed being just one of the guys.

"He was a great freshman," coach Wally Goodwin said of Tiger. "He's the best kid I have ever known. He's a better kid than he is a player. I have a world of admiration for that youngster. I will never meet another one like him."

STANFORD UNIVERSITY

Many people consider Stanford University the finest school in California. The university was founded in 1891 in Stanford, California, about thirty miles south of San Francisco. The team nickname for Stanford is the Cardinal, which refers to the bright red in the school's colors.

While Tiger was just another freshman off the course, he was nothing like the other freshmen, or anybody else, on it. His first college tournament was the Tucker Invitational in Albuquerque, New Mexico. Tiger won the event with a score of 68, four strokes under par. Even against some of the best college golfers in the country, Tiger was in a league of his own.

Not everything was going well, though. Tiger's fame had grown, and that wasn't always a good thing. He received a few racist letters and threats. Some people didn't like that an African American player was on pace to become one of the best golfers in the world. But Tiger tried not to let those people bother him. He remembered that the best way he could fight their racism was to keep winning and to continue being a gentleman on and off the course.

Tiger had a chance to confront racism on the golf course in October 1994. Stanford took part in the Jerry Pate Invitational in Shoal Creek, near Birmingham, Alabama. A few years earlier, a news story had appeared about how the club refused to take African American members. Tiger knew that if he could win a tournament there, it would make a strong statement for the African American community.

Some African Americans from nearby Birmingham didn't agree. They thought Tiger should refuse to play in the tournament. But Tiger didn't want to turn his back on his teammates. Despite protestors at the event, he remained calm and won the tournament. Winning was his way of protesting the club's actions.

Tiger had once again found immediate success at a new level. In his first year, he was named the Pac-10 conference's Player of the Year. The Pacific 10, or Pac-10, is Stanford's athletic conference. It includes ten of the biggest universities in the western United States. Tiger was also named to the National Collegiate Athletic Association's (NCAA's) All-American team.

Tiger's 1994 U.S. Amateur win opened many doors, including a chance to play in the Masters in the spring of 1995. Tiger would play the tournament as an amateur, and while he wouldn't be paid for his finish, it was still his first chance to play in one of golf's major tournaments, or majors. Playing and winning in the Masters, the U.S. Open, the British Open, and the PGA Championship define a golfer's career.

Tiger was no ordinary player. Only a few amateurs are even allowed to play in the Masters. At age nineteen, Tiger was the youngest. He was also the first African American to play in the event since Lee Elder in the 1970s.

Tiger spent months preparing for the Masters. He watched old videotapes of past Masters to see how the pros played their shots. Because the Masters is held at Augusta National Golf Club every year, unlike the other majors, Tiger had a chance to see how top golfers approached the course year after year. He studied every hole, noting which kinds of shots got golfers into trouble and which kinds of shots led to birdies.

> **❝** *If you are up there week-in and week-out with your chances to win, you'll win. You're not going to win every one, but you'll win.* **❞**
>
> —TIGER WOODS

The tournament started on a rainy Thursday morning. A large crowd gathered to watch Tiger's first tee shot. Tiger didn't disappoint, hitting a long, straight shot down the fairway. But his approach left him with a tough downhill shot, which sailed past the hole. He ended the hole with a bogey. It wasn't the start he had wanted.

At the end of his first round, Tiger had an even-par 72. It wasn't a great round, but he was still in good shape to make the cut.

Tiger posted the same score on Friday. Again it wasn't a great round, but it was good enough. He had made the cut. If he could play two great rounds on Saturday and Sunday, he could be in position to challenge for a win. But that hope disappeared on Saturday, when he shot a five-over 77. Tiger wasn't going to win his first major. He recovered to shoot another 72 on Sunday, finishing forty-first overall.

Tiger returned to Stanford after his final round. He didn't have too much time to look back on his first Masters, though.

He had to start studying immediately for a history test the next day.

In May Tiger tied for eighteenth place at the NCAA West Regionals, and two weeks later he finished the NCAA Championships tied for fifth place. Jack Nicklaus had won the NCAA Championships while at Ohio State University, and Tiger wanted to make sure he had a win to match that one before he was through with college.

JACK NICKLAUS

From the beginning, Tiger has measured his success against that of golf's greatest player, Jack Nicklaus. Nicklaus became a professional in 1961. In 1962, he won the U.S. Open and was named Rookie of the Year. His best year may have been 1972, when he won seven events, including the Masters and the U.S. Open.

Over his career, Nicklaus won seventy-three PGA Tour events, including eighteen majors. He was named the PGA Player of the Year five times. At the 2004 Memorial Tournament, the sixty-four-year-old Nicklaus became the oldest golfer to ever make the cut in a PGA event.

Tiger entered the summer of 1995 with several goals. One goal was to play in more professional tournaments, where he could compete against and learn from the best golfers in the world. His biggest goal, though, was to win a second U.S. Amateur title.

A week after Tiger finished his final exams at Stanford, he went to Shinnecock Hills Golf Course in Southampton, New York, for the U.S. Open. He quickly discovered that the powerful game he used in the Masters wasn't going to help him in the U.S. Open. The course demanded that golfers play shorter, safer shots. Hitting for distance usually just got Tiger into trouble. His shots often missed the fairway, and his score kept climbing. On the second day, as he tried to save one of his missed shots, he hurt his wrist. He had to take himself out of the tournament.

Tiger's wrist needed several weeks to heal. He missed a few amateur tournaments, but his next big event was the British Open. Tiger had some trouble with the wide-open course at St. Andrews in Scotland. St. Andrews is a links course, which means it's set on open, rolling land. Links courses have few trees. They don't require the fine targeting of most American golf courses. Instead players must know how to play slopes and handle strong winds. Tiger shot one stroke over par for the first two days but still made the cut. In the tournament, he never really adapted to links golf, and he finished a distant sixty-eighth.

Tiger wasn't happy with his finishes in the professional tournaments, but the event that really mattered to him was the U.S. Amateur. In 1995 the event was held at the Newport

Country Club in Newport, Rhode Island. The tournament didn't start well for Tiger. He missed several easy shots the first day but still managed a score of 68, two under par. The second day was much worse. His driving was bad and his putts weren't falling. He finished with a five-over score of 75. His hopes of defending his U.S. Amateur title almost died right there. But he barely made the cut and advanced to match play.

Tiger quickly fixed the problems he was having and dominated match play the way only he could. None of his first five opponents ever even held a lead.

George "Buddy" Marucci Jr. joined Tiger in the thirty-six-hole final match. Marucci took an early three-hole lead, but Tiger quickly erased it. The two golfers stayed close through most of the match, neither able to pull away.

By the final hole, Tiger was one up. When Marucci hit a nice second shot onto the green, the pressure was on. Tiger stood on the fairway, sizing up the shot, knowing that this was his chance to win the tournament and avoid a playoff. He gripped his eight iron and took a strong swing. The ball sailed into the air and landed beyond the pin. It spun backward and stopped less than a foot and a half from the hole. Tiger pumped his fist as the crowd cheered.

After Marucci missed his birdie putt, he conceded the hole and the championship. He didn't seem too upset. He spoke highly of his opponent, saying, "I can live with losing to Tiger."

Tiger returned to Stanford, where he enjoyed another successful year both on the golf course and in the classroom. He enjoyed learning about economics, and he hoped the knowledge would help him manage the money he planned to win on the PGA Tour. He also continued lifting weights, working to become even stronger and more powerful.

Tiger's win in the 1995 U.S. Amateur earned him a place in the 1996 Masters. Again he flew to Augusta, Georgia, for golf's greatest event. This time, Tiger knew the course and felt more comfortable. His game had improved over the last year, and he believed that he could avoid some of the mistakes he'd made previously.

❝ *I've never played well during school, because I'm not focusing on golf, I'm focusing on school. The only time I play well is the summer.* **❞**

—TIGER WOODS

However, the pressure on Tiger had also increased. People were already talking about when he might leave the amateur ranks behind to join the PGA Tour. All the buildup may have been too much for the college student. Tiger's first round was a disappointing 75, three strokes over par. The second round wasn't any better, and Tiger missed the cut. It was a rare step backward for a golfer who was used to sprinting forward.

Tiger returned to Stanford, where he prepared for the Pac-10 Championships at Big Canyon Country Club in Newport Beach, California. The tournament started on April 29, and that day Tiger played some of the best golf of his life, at any level. In the morning round, he shot an amazing 61, eleven strokes under par, shattering the course record of 66. In the late round, he shot a seven-under 65, putting him a total of eighteen strokes under par. In one day, he had given himself a fourteen-stroke lead. He cruised to the win the next day.

Tiger's hot play continued in the NCAA West Regionals, where he won and advanced to the NCAA Championships. He was one step away from conquering yet another golf title. Only Jack Nicklaus and Phil Mickelson had won the NCAA Championships and the U.S. Amateur in the same year.

This kid is the most fundamentally sound golfer I've seen at any age. And he's a nice kid. He's got great composure. . . . He will be your favorite for the next twenty years. If he isn't, there's something wrong.

—JACK NICKLAUS

The NCAA Championships began on May 29 at the Honors Course in Chattanooga, Tennessee. Tiger shot an impressive 69 on the first day, three strokes under par. He was even better in the second round, breaking the course record with a score of 67. His third-round score of 69 gave him a huge lead, and, despite a disappointing score of 80 in the final round, he easily beat second-place Rory Sabbatini.

Tiger had only one goal left as an amateur. He wanted to do what no other golfer had done—win a third-straight U.S. Amateur.

Chapter Five

Turning Pro

When Tiger left Stanford for the summer in 1996, he said that he planned to go back to school unless something dramatic happened. His sights were set on the U.S. Amateur, but he also planned to play in both the U.S. Open and the British Open as an amateur.

Tiger started the U.S. Open well. He was paired with John Daly, and together they were two of the longest-hitting golfers in the tournament. Tiger took advantage of his power early and actually shared the lead for a short time after he birdied the 12th hole. But the good start didn't last. Two holes later, his ball rolled behind a drain near the green and forced him into making a bad chip. Everything got worse from there. By the time the round was over, he was six strokes over par. In the last five holes alone, he was nine strokes over. His hopes of winning the U.S. Open were dashed.

The British Open was a chance for Tiger to make up for his first-round collapse at the U.S. Open. Again he struggled in his opening round, shooting four strokes over par. But on the second day, Tiger found his swing. He shot five under par, then finished with back-to-back rounds of one under. Tiger finished the tournament in twenty-sixth place and won the Silver Medal, the prize given to the amateur who has the highest finish in the event. Tiger was happy to have done well, although he still wanted to win. Most important, the good finish showed him that he was ready to compete as a professional.

After the British Open, Tiger talked to Butch Harmon, his longtime personal coach. Before the event, Harmon had encouraged Tiger to return to school. But after the British Open, even Harmon thought that maybe Tiger was ready.

But before he could turn pro, Tiger had one more thing he wanted to do. Winning a third-straight U.S. Amateur would be the perfect way to end his amateur career. He would have nothing else left to accomplish.

In the opening rounds of the U.S. Amateur, Tiger shot 69 and 67, leaving no doubt who was the best golfer on the course. His was the best score of the tournament, and he easily advanced to match play.

Tiger advanced smoothly through his first several matches. By now, his legend had grown so large that many of his opponents were happy just to lose to him. His third-round opponent, Charles Howell, said, "I didn't lose 10 and 8, so I'm happy. He's awesome."

In the semifinal match, Tiger faced Stanford teammate Joel Kribel. Kribel knew Tiger and wasn't intimidated the way many other players were. Kribel played well and was two up through the first nine holes.

On the tenth hole, Tiger found himself in danger after he had driven himself into the bunker. He couldn't afford to go down three holes. Tiger made a great shot out of the sand and saved the hole, keeping himself in the match.

The shot turned around Tiger's day. He dominated the back nine with two birdies and an eagle and defeated his friend and teammate 3 and 1. Only nineteen-year-old Steve Scott and thirty-six holes stood between Tiger and a third-straight title.

Scott proved to be Tiger's toughest competition of the tournament. He had Tiger five down at one point, but Tiger came back strong. By the time the golfers went to the thirty-fifth hole, Scott's lead was down to one.

Tiger's chances looked fairly dim after a bad approach shot left him an incredibly difficult thirty-five-foot putt over an uneven green. Tiger stood over the ball, measured the green, and calmly sank one of the most difficult putts of the entire tournament. "That's a feeling I'll remember for the rest of my life," Tiger later said of the putt.

After tying on the thirty-sixth hole, the players entered a sudden-death play-off. They would play until someone won a hole, and then the match would be over. Tiger had a scare on the first hole when Scott had an eighteen-foot putt for the title. But Scott missed the shot and the match continued.

GOLFING HEROES

Tiger idolized many golfers as he grew up, but two of the golfers he most respected were Charlie Sifford and Lee Elder. In 1967 Sifford became the first African American golfer to win a PGA Tour event. In 1975 Elder became the first African American to play in the Masters.

Both Sifford and Elder played during a time when many golf courses didn't allow African Americans to play. They faced a great deal of racism to play their sport. Tiger gives them both credit for where he is today.

On the next hole, Tiger hit a beautiful six-iron shot to within twelve feet of the hole. He missed his putt but tapped in the next shot for par and the championship. Tiger hugged his parents, celebrating the historic accomplishment.

"That was probably the best Amateur final match ever," Scott said. "Just to be a part of it, I feel completely a winner."

Tiger celebrated his victory knowing that it was the end of that part of his life. He wouldn't be going for a fourth-straight title. He wouldn't be returning to defend his NCAA championship. He had nothing left to accomplish as an amateur. He was going pro.

Just two days later, on August 28, 1996, twenty-year-old Tiger called a press conference. There he announced his plans to the world. "I had intended to stay in school, play four years at Stanford, and get my degree, but things change," he said. "I didn't know my game was going to progress to this point. . . . Winning the third Amateur in a row is a great way to go out. I always said I would know when it was time, and now is the time."

The next PGA Tour event, the Greater Milwaukee Open, started the next day. Tiger announced that he would be entering the tournament as a professional.

Once Tiger made his announcement, things happened quickly. Tiger would begin making money for the tournaments he played, but that was almost an afterthought. He was already the biggest name in golf, and companies wanted him to endorse their products. Nike and Titleist immediately signed Tiger to multimillion-dollar deals. Tiger was finally going to get a chance to use the accounting and economics education he'd received in his two years at Stanford.

Tiger was happy about the money, but the little extras made him even more excited. Titleist sent him several boxes of golf balls and some gloves. Nike sent clothing and bags. Some people said that Tiger was more interested in the free equipment than he was in the money.

The week had already been exhausting, but Tiger went to Milwaukee, thrilled to be playing his first match as a professional. The Greater Milwaukee Open normally would have been a small tournament without much media attention, but Tiger's arrival changed all of that. Media members and fans swarmed the tournament, all wanting to see Tiger in his first time out as a professional. The ESPN television network broadcast the first two rounds of the event, and the announcers admitted that Tiger was the only reason they were there. The last two rounds aired on ABC.

THE NIKE CONNECTION

Tiger developed a friendship with basketball legend Michael Jordan. Both athletes had big endorsement deals with Nike. Jordan was older, and he understood what Tiger was going through. The men formed a tight bond.

Jordan, a huge golf fan, was amazed at what Tiger could do on the course. He was always happy to play a round.

Tiger didn't disappoint the crowds on his first day. He ripped a 336-yard drive straight down the fairway on his first shot as a pro, sending the crowd into a frenzy. He built on the early success, playing well in all areas of his game and finishing with a score of 67, four strokes under par. "It was great just to get back to what I do, play golf," Tiger said after his round.

 Tiger moved to Orlando, Florida, when he turned professional. Florida has no state income tax, and Tiger knew the move would save him millions of dollars. Tiger can also golf whenever he wants to—Isleworth Country Club is less than a mile from his house! He even moved in next to another PGA star, Mark O'Meara.

If Tiger was exhausted from his week, it didn't show in his second round, either, where he shot a solid two under 69, good enough to make the cut. But the long week finally caught up with him during his third round on Saturday. Tiger played poorly and finished with a score of 73, two strokes over par, taking him out of competition for the title. Tiger shot a 68 on the last day and finished in a distant tie for sixtieth. His first paycheck from a PGA event was for $2,544. It wasn't much, especially compared to the millions he was making in endorsements, but it meant he had arrived.

Tiger had no time to rest. His plan was to play in six events in six weeks. He needed to win enough prize money to rank among the top 125 golfers on the tour. If he could achieve that goal, he would earn "exempt" status for all of the Tour events in 1997. Players with exempt status are automatically qualified. All they have to do to play in the tournament is show up.

Tiger's next PGA event was the Canadian Open, where he finished eleventh. He then went to the Quad Cities Classic, where his fantastic second-round score of 64 gave him a lead. Tiger held that lead heading into the final day, his first real chance to win a PGA Tour event.

Tiger's hopes began to disappear with a terrible fourth hole. His drive sailed into a pond; he then bounced his next shot off a tree and back into the water. Rattled, Tiger needed four more strokes to sink a putt, finishing with a disastrous quadruple bogey. He finished the tournament in fifth place. It was his first top-ten finish, but it was hard to be happy about his play in that last round.

The B.C. Open was Tiger's fourth tournament as a professional. Again he played well in the early rounds and was near the top of the leader board entering the final day. He hoped for a win, but wet weather and a few bad shots left him in third at the end of the day. Tiger's finishes were getting better and better with each tournament he played. He was quickly climbing the PGA Tour's money list, and his goal of ranking among the top 125 was in sight.

Tiger's next tournament was the Buick Challenge in Pine Mountain, Georgia. It was going to be a busy week. He was also planning to attend a dinner where he would receive an award as the top college golfer from the previous year.

From his warm-up tournaments early in the summer to his emotional U.S. Amateur victory, Tiger had been strong. His first week as a professional had been a whirlwind of activity, and he hadn't let up since. As he waited in Pine Mountain for the Buick Challenge to begin, Tiger felt overwhelmed and exhausted. Suddenly playing golf and dealing with fans and the media seemed like more than he wanted to handle. He needed a break.

Tiger pulled himself out of the tournament and decided not to attend the dinner. Right away, people questioned his decision. They said he was immature. They wondered about his character, saying that he should honor his commitments. Even Tiger's fellow golfers criticized his choice.

"Tiger should have played," said golf legend Arnold Palmer. "He should have gone to the dinner. You don't make commitments you can't fulfill unless you are on your deathbed, and I don't believe he was."

Tiger wasn't sorry for backing out of the tournament, but he realized that he had made a mistake by not attending the dinner. He apologized to everyone who had planned to attend the dinner.

> ❝I thought these people were my friends. . . . I'm a target for everybody now, and there's nothing I can do about it. My mother was right when she said that turning pro would take away my youth. But golfwise, there was nothing left for me in college.❞
>
> —TIGER WOODS

With the worst of the criticism behind him and some much-needed rest, Tiger was ready to return to the Tour. It was time people started talking again about his play on the course, not his behavior off it.

Chapter Six

Hunting for a Win

After Tiger had blown his lead in the Quad Cities Classic several weeks earlier, Earl Woods had told friends that Tiger's big day would come at the Las Vegas Invitational, which began on Wednesday, October 2. It was a bigger event than most of the tournaments Tiger had played in since turning pro, and both father and son had a feeling that it might be special for Tiger.

Tiger was rested and ready, eager to put the controversy of the Buick Challenge behind him for good. Still, early in the tournament, it didn't look like Earl's prediction was going to come true. Tiger shot a two-under score of 70 in the first round, placing him a distant eight strokes behind the leaders. Tiger's score would have been good in many tournaments, but the Las Vegas Invitational was played on three courses that were all fairly easy for skilled golfers. Two under wasn't nearly good enough. But another part of the Las Vegas Invitational separates it from most other events—it takes place over five rounds instead of the usual four. Tiger had an extra round to make up for his bad day.

This was a bit of Las Vegas luck that Tiger didn't intend to waste. While many of the other golfers went to Las Vegas's casinos after their rounds, twenty-year-old Tiger wasn't allowed to gamble. All he could do was plan for the next round.

Despite some troubles putting, Tiger improved greatly on Thursday, shooting a nine-under 63. It was the best round of his young professional career. But he still trailed the leaders by seven strokes.

HURTING IN VEGAS

Despite Tiger's great performance in the Las Vegas Invitational, he wasn't completely healthy. During Friday's round, he aggravated a groin injury he had suffered weeks earlier at the U.S. Amateur. He limped a bit, and people could see pain in his face as he hit several shots on Sunday.

Tiger played well on Friday and Saturday, shooting rounds of 68 and 67. He was smashing the ball, hitting long, straight drives that nobody else in the field could match. For the tournament, his drives averaged 323 yards. The next-longest hitter was John Adams, who averaged 310 yards. The average drive for the whole field was 285 yards, putting Tiger a whopping 38 yards ahead.

Despite his good scores and booming drives, Tiger was still having trouble erasing the deficit he had given himself after the first round. With only one round left, he was still tied for seventh place, four strokes behind leader Ronnie Black.

At the first tee on Sunday, Tiger stood determined and ready. He still had a long way to come back, but he was confident. He'd made big comebacks before. He quickly showed the crowd that he wasn't going to go away, sinking a fifteen-foot birdie putt on the first green.

On the 11th hole, Tiger hit his tee shot into a sand trap, but he wasn't discouraged. He hit a perfect shot with his sand wedge to put him on the green with a thirty-foot putt. He sank the putt and scored a birdie.

Tiger was so strong Sunday that he sometimes got himself in trouble. On the 15th hole, a par four, he used a three wood to shoot for the green. He crushed the ball, which sailed 315 yards into a sand trap *behind* the green. Tiger was hitting shots with his three wood longer than most golfers were hitting them with their drivers.

Tiger dropped his putt on the 18th hole to finish the day with a score of 64. Davis Love III, who had taken the lead earlier, was still on the course finishing his round. Tiger could only wait. He went to a practice tee and kept swinging to stay loose, knowing that a playoff was possible.

TIGER'S TRAINING

When Tiger first joined the PGA Tour, his devotion to off-course training set him apart from most of the other players on the Tour. The strength and flexibility Tiger developed in his workouts was one reason he could outdrive nearly all of the other pros. Of course, other golfers soon learned to follow Tiger's example, and weight lifting and stretching have since become common practice for nearly all golfers.

Love had a chance for a birdie putt to win the event on the 18th hole, but he missed it, forcing a playoff. The two golfers would continue playing until one of them won a hole. Tiger was ready. Love had been one of the golfers who had criticized Tiger for leaving the Buick Challenge earlier, and now the men faced off in a sudden-death playoff for the title. Celebrating his first PGA Tour win would be a perfect way for Tiger to put the Buick Challenge behind him.

The two golfers returned to the tee of the 18th hole for the playoff. Both men hit straight fairway shots off the tee. Tiger's second shot landed softly on the green, about eighteen feet from the hole. The pressure was on Love, who overshot the hole and landed in a sand trap about six feet from the hole. Knowing Love had a tough shot, Tiger made a safe putt, then tapped in a two-footer for par. The pressure was on Love, who had a chance to force another playoff hole with a six-foot putt. But Love missed the putt and the tournament was over.

> ❝ He thinks about winning and nothing else. I like the way he thinks. We were all trying to prolong the inevitable. We knew he was going to win. I just didn't want it to be today. Everybody better watch out: He's going to be a force. ❞
>
> —DAVIS LOVE III

The crowd roared. Tiger smiled and shook Love's hand, then turned to hug his mother. He was pleased with the win, but when he talked, he suggested that it had taken him too long. "It should've come at Quad City," he said. "I learned a lot from that."

Tiger had achieved two more goals. He had won a PGA event, and he had also assured himself a place among the PGA Tour's top 125 money winners for the year. He no longer had to worry about qualifying for tournaments in 1997. His golfing life had just gotten a whole lot easier.

> ❝I'm surprised it took this long. I'm one of the few people who really knew how good he is. For him, to just be able to play golf was the key.❞
>
> —TIGER'S COACH, BUTCH HARMON

The next week, Tiger continued his good play at the Texas Open, where he finished third, only two strokes behind winner David Ogrin. Third place was still a great finish for the twenty-year-old, but he wanted to win.

Tiger didn't feel well the following week at the Walt Disney World Classic in Lake Buena Vista, Florida, just outside Orlando. He shot a 69 in the opening round. That evening, he told his father that he needed to shoot a 63 the next day, and that's exactly what he did.

On Saturday, Tiger shot a 69. It wasn't a great score, but it was enough to keep him among the leaders entering the final day. Tiger's playing partner for the last round was Payne Stewart, one of the best golfers on the PGA Tour. Both men were having great final rounds. Stewart shot a 67 for the day, putting the pressure on Tiger to play flawlessly. Tiger responded with a 66. Another golfer, Taylor Smith, would have tied Tiger for first place, but PGA officials discovered that Smith had accidentally used an illegal putter during his round.

Tiger holds the 1994 U.S. Amateur Championship trophy. He went on to win the event again in 1995 and 1996, becoming the first person to win it three times in a row.

Tiger's parents, Earl *(left)* and Kultida *(center)*, study his moves at the 2002 Masters. They, along with his future wife, Elin Nordegren *(right)*, all wear red, Tiger's lucky color.

Tiger is eager to break the records set by golf legend Jack Nicklaus *(right)*.

At the 2003 British Open, Tiger finds himself in the rough.

A large crowd always gathers when Tiger steps up to the tee.

Tiger arrives in Germany to play in the 2003 Deutsche Bank Open. World travel is a normal part of this superstar's schedule.

Caddie Steve Williams stands watch as Tiger lines up his putt.

Tiger pumps his fist in celebration after making a birdie putt during the third round of the 2005 Buick Invitational. He went on to win the tournament the following day.

Smith was disqualified, and Tiger was alone in first. This time, he didn't need a playoff to come out on top. It was his second win in three weeks.

 Tiger's winnings for the Las Vegas Invitational totaled $297,000. For winning the Walt Disney World Classic, he earned $216,000.

If anyone in the golf world didn't already know, the win in Florida sent a powerful message. Tiger Woods had arrived. Golf would never be the same.

Chapter Seven

Highs and Lows

Tiger's amazing start on the PGA Tour didn't go unnoticed. For years, he had been a celebrity in the golf world. Now he was truly a household name. Fans flocked to his tournaments. PGA events had never seen such crowds. Many people called it "Tigermania." For years, golf's popularity had been in a slow decline. All by himself, Tiger changed that.

"To look out here and see so many kids, I think that's wonderful," Tiger said of the change. "They see someone they can relate to, me being so young. It's really nice seeing more minorities in the gallery. I think that's where the game should go and will go."

As 1996 drew to a close, Tiger was showered with attention and awards. *Sports Illustrated* named him Sportsman of the Year, one of the highest honors in sports. He also won the PGA Tour's Rookie of the Year Award as the sport's best first-year player. More and more companies asked Tiger to endorse their products. In less than a year, Tiger had already become one of the richest athletes in history.

All the attention didn't slow Tiger down a bit. His first event of the 1997 season was the Mercedes Championships in Carlsbad, California. After three rounds, Tiger was tied for the lead with Tom Lehman, the PGA Tour's leading money winner from 1996.

In 1997 Tiger shot an amazing score of 59 in a practice round at Isleworth Country Club in Orlando, Florida. At thirteen under par, his score set the course record.

Even Lehman knew how tough Tiger would be to beat. "I'm not sure if I feel like the underdog or what," he said after Saturday's round. "It's almost like trying to hold off the inevitable, like bailing water out of a sinking boat."

Bad weather prevented the event from continuing on Sunday. Only one hole on the course was in good enough shape to play. Tournament officials decided that Tiger and Lehman would have a sudden-death playoff on that hole. They would keep playing it until one of them was ahead.

Lehman had the first shot. He stood over the ball and pulled back his six iron. But his swing was wild, and the ball went into a pond. Tiger's tee shot sailed high in the sky and came down on the green, inches from the pin. He had almost hit a hole in one. The playoff was over that quickly.

Tiger was pleased with his wins and with his popularity. But his goals had once again shifted. He had played in several majors as an amateur but had never really had a chance to win one. As a professional, he'd quickly become the man to beat. When the Masters rolled around in April, Tiger was ready to win it.

CHAMPION'S DINNER

Even with his huge Masters victory, Tiger couldn't just focus on golf. The Masters champion gets to choose a menu at a celebration dinner. PGA Tour veteran Fuzzy Zoeller said that he hoped Tiger wouldn't serve fried chicken or collard greens or "whatever . . . *they* serve."

Many people were shocked at Zoeller's racist comments. Tiger held his head high and refused to get into a war of words. For his dinner, he chose a menu that included his favorite foods—cheeseburgers, french fries, chicken sandwiches, and milk shakes.

In the trademark victory of Tiger's young career, he became the youngest golfer to win the Masters. His dominating twelve-stroke victory stunned the golf world and once again proved that when his game was on, he was in a league of his own. Tigermania had been big before, but suddenly, it was everywhere.

"The rest of us never had a chance to win," second-place finisher Tom Kite said. "And we might not ever have another chance if he keeps his head on his shoulders."

Tiger won two more tournaments in 1997, the Byron Nelson Golf Classic and the Western Open. His game, at times, still needed work. He was only twenty-one years old and hadn't yet learned to perform at his highest level all of the time.

In September, Tiger traveled to Spain to play in the Ryder Cup, one of golf's few team events. The Ryder Cup takes place once every two years and features the best golfers from the United States playing against the best golfers from Europe. The Ryder Cup isn't a PGA Tour event. Golfers don't compete for cash prizes. They play for pride and patriotism. The format of the Ryder Cup is also unlike that of any other golf tournament. For the first few days, players play with partners. They work together to win points for the team. Each match is worth a point. In a tie, each team is awarded half a point.

Mark O'Meara was Tiger's partner. On Friday, they won their first match but lost the second. They lost another match on

Saturday morning. On Saturday afternoon, Tiger and his new partner, Justin Leonard, earned a tie. Tiger was frustrated with his play. Several of his putts rolled around the edge of the hole but didn't go in. At the end of the day, the European team held a 10.5–5.5 lead.

The event didn't get any better for Tiger on Sunday, when he lost his singles match to Italian Costantino Rocca. Tiger's failure was especially hard for him to take because the American team almost erased the European team's lead. In the end, the European team won 14.5–13.5. If Tiger could have just won his singles match, the American team would have won the Ryder Cup. It was difficult for Tiger, who had been such a strong match player throughout his amateur career.

 Fishing is one of Tiger's favorite hobbies. He owns more than fifteen fishing rods. Tiger's favorite places to fish include Alaska and Ireland.

His failure at the Ryder Cup was one of the few truly bad events for Tiger in 1997. Overall, his first season as a profes-sional had been a tremendous success. He led the Tour in win-nings at more than $2 million. He also moved up to the number one ranking among all golfers. A golfer's rank is based on the average number of points he's earned per tournament during the previous two years. Each golf tournament is worth a certain number of points, and the more recent tournaments are weighted to count more than the earlier events. At the end of the season, the PGA voted him Player of the Year. In addition, the Associated Press named him Male Athlete of the Year.

Not everyone was happy with Tiger, though. He had trouble dealing with reporters. After a bad day on the course, Tiger would refuse to talk with them. Some media members said that he was too arrogant, that he only wanted to use the media when things were going well. Some of Tiger's fellow players also grumbled about the young star. They thought that he didn't work hard enough. Tiger even managed to make headlines by declining an invitation to the White House from President Bill Clinton. Tiger wanted to go on vacation instead. Many players and fans became impatient with the young star.

Tiger headed into the 1998 season with all the momentum in the world. Every year, his game had improved dramatically. He had no reason to believe 1998 would be any different. His four victories in 1997 had been impressive. People wondered how many he might win in 1998, with another year of experience under his belt.

He started the year looking like he'd be better than ever. He finished second to Phil Mickelson in the year's opening event, the Mercedes Championships. Then in the Johnnie Walker Classic in Thailand, he made an amazing comeback from eight strokes down on the final day. He shot a stunning 65, seven strokes under par, forcing a play-off with Ernie Els. On the second play-off hole, Tiger sank a fourteen-foot birdie putt to win the match.

Tiger scored top-five finishes in his next two events. He looked ready to dominate another season. But somewhere along the way, Tiger got off his track. Suddenly his drives weren't as straight or weren't hit as far. His approach shots didn't have their same pinpoint accuracy. Putts that he usually sank came up short or rimmed out. Tiger won only one more PGA event in 1998, the Bellsouth Classic. He had a chance at another win in the British Open but finished third, one stroke behind Mark O'Meara and Brian Watts. O'Meara went on to win in a playoff.

After Tiger's amazing debut in 1996 and his dominating season in 1997, many people wondered if anyone could challenge him. But after 1998, Tiger Woods suddenly looked human. He wasn't going to win every week. Like everyone else, he was going to have to work harder to improve his game.

Tiger still had his list of Jack Nicklaus's accomplishments. As he looked at it after the 1998 season, he knew he was falling behind. Nicklaus had won three of his first eight majors as a professional. The 1997 Masters was still Tiger's only major victory in eight tries as a pro. Tiger had work to do.

Chapter | Eight

Back on Track

Tiger had something to prove after his disappointing performance in 1998. He started off 1999 with a bang. He finished in the top five in five of his first six events, including a win at the Buick Invitational, where, over four days, he shot a fantastic twenty-two under par.

Tiger's hot start didn't last. He had a disappointing spring, which included an eighteenth-place finish at the Masters. Tiger lost his number one ranking to David Duval, and he was hungry for a win.

The cold streak didn't last long. As the summer of 1999 settled in, so did Tiger's game. He was about to begin one of the best runs of golf of his life. Tiger's hot play began at the Deutsche Bank Open in Heidelberg, Germany, where he fought for a three-stroke win over South African player Retief Goosen. The tournament wasn't a part of the PGA Tour, but it was still an important win for him at a time when his confidence was low. His good play continued two weeks later in his next PGA Tour event, the Memorial Tournament.

Often Tiger's long drives and great putting ability had won him tournaments. At the Memorial, his short game was the key. In his final round, his driving was wild. He missed many of the fairways. But he hit great second shots that allowed him to save par and hold his lead. One of his best shots came on the 14th hole, where he had misplayed his approach shot and was stuck in the rough off the putting surface. Tiger made a short chip shot that cleared the rough and rolled downhill, straight for the pin. The ball dropped into the hole, once again saving par. Tiger's final-round score of 69 wasn't his best of the tournament, but his ability to make the best of a bad day gave him his second win in a row. Tiger was on a roll.

❝ *If you were building the complete golfer, you'd build Tiger Woods.* **❞**

—MARK O'MEARA

Two weeks later, Tiger entered the U.S. Open. It was a tournament he'd never won, and he felt like he had a great chance. Despite bad weather, Tiger started off well with a two-under score of 68 for the first round. He stayed among the leaders for the entire event. By the last day, Tiger was chasing leader Payne Stewart. He had a chance to pull within a stroke of the lead on the 11th hole, but he missed a twelve-foot putt for birdie, then carelessly missed his next two-foot putt. The bogey dropped him three strokes behind Stewart.

Tiger didn't quit. He sank a twenty-foot putt on the 14th hole, dropping to his knees as the ball went in. He still had a chance. After he birdied the very difficult 16th hole, he was only one stroke behind, with two holes to play. But the 17th hole was another disaster for Tiger. First he hit his tee shot into the sand. Then he missed a five-foot putt that would have saved par. He ended up with a bogey, and Stewart won the title. Tiger finished third.

"I know I can win a Masters, I know I can win a British Open, because I've come close," Tiger said. "It makes me feel like I can definitely win a U.S. Open. I know I have the game, I know I have the mind. It's just a matter of time."

Tiger didn't let his near miss at the U.S. Open get him down. His next tournament was the Western Open near Chicago, Illinois. While in Chicago, Tiger had a chance to spend time with his friend Michael Jordan. By the time the tournament started, Tiger was relaxed and ready to win. He had a share of the lead after two rounds, then held on for a three-stroke win, his third victory in his last four events. It was an important win because Tiger wanted to enter the next event on a good note. He'd gone nine straight majors without a win, and he wanted to end that streak at his next event, the British Open.

Tiger didn't get his wish. Just as in the U.S. Open the previous month, several bad putts left him in seventh place by the end of the event. His streak grew to ten straight majors without a win. Tiger prided himself on being a clutch performer, an athlete who plays his best in the biggest, most important events. He had shown in his amateur career that he responded well to pressure. But suddenly, he found himself missing short putts and making mental errors during the biggest tournaments.

Overall, the year 1999 had been a good one for Tiger, but it wouldn't be complete without a major victory. His last chance came in August at the PGA Championship in Medinah, Illinois.

A Rivalry Is Born

In 1999 a nineteen-year-old Spanish golfer named Sergio Garcia began to make a name for himself on the PGA Tour. He was the first young golfer to take any real attention away from Tiger. Garcia stood only five feet, ten inches tall and weighed barely 150 pounds. His fans called him "El Niño," Spanish for "The Boy." Garcia's favorite slogan was *Suerte o Muerte,* which means "luck or death."

He started with a two-under score of 70 in the first round, which put him four strokes behind the leader, a nineteen-year-old newcomer named Sergio Garcia.

Tiger played great golf on Friday and Saturday, ripping powerful, straight drives and taking advantage of the course's long fairways. His scores of 67 and 68 moved him into the lead, two strokes ahead of Garcia and Stewart Cink. After Saturday's round, Garcia said, "If he keeps playing like he played today, maybe we will have to look for second place."

At first, it looked like second place was exactly what Garcia was playing for. Tiger's lead swelled early. The other competitors quickly faded on Sunday, leaving only Garcia to challenge Tiger, who held a five-stroke advantage with seven holes remaining.

But then, everything seemed to change. Tiger made a few bad shots, while Garcia came on strong. The young challenger's confidence grew. On the 13th hole, Garcia ripped a perfect drive, then hit a fifteen-foot putt to put the pressure on Tiger, who was waiting to tee off on the same hole. Garcia gave Tiger a long, challenging stare, then tipped his hat.

Tiger missed his chance to answer Garcia's challenge, though. He hit a bad tee shot, then fumbled with his short game. He scored a double bogey on the hole, and suddenly his lead had all but disappeared.

The crowd continued to cheer for Garcia, chanting, "SER-GI-O, SER-GI-O!" The fans loved the young golfer's attitude and enthusiasm. Tiger wasn't used to hearing the crowd cheer so loudly for anyone other than him. But he didn't let it affect his game.

The average speed of the club head during one of Tiger's swings is 125 miles per hour. An average golfer's speed is about 84 miles per hour.

Tiger's lead was down to a single stroke on the final two holes. On the 17th, he pulled a seven iron from his bag and stepped up to tee off. He crushed the ball, which sailed far over the green and landed in deep rough. He made a poor chip shot from the rough and still had a tough eight-foot putt to save par and hold onto his lead. Tiger read the slope of the green, knowing the ball would fall from left to right. He aimed, stroked the ball, and watched as it curved right into the hole. Tiger pumped his fist in celebration. He had kept the pressure on Garcia. If the youngster was going to force a playoff, Tiger wanted to make him earn it with a birdie.

Tiger calmly sank another par putt on the 18th hole and waited. Garcia missed a birdie putt on the 17th green, then set himself up with another putt to tie the match on the last hole. Tiger watched as Garcia missed the putt, sighing with relief as he realized the tournament was over. Tiger's winless streak in the majors had ended. He'd won his first PGA Championship. Exhausted, Tiger said, "To come out of it on top took everything out of me. I just tried to hold him off and did the best I could."

The PGA Championship was the highlight of Tiger's great 1999 season, but it wasn't the end of it. After a disappointing thirty-seventh place finish in the Sprint International, Tiger won the NEC Invitational.

Next Tiger and his American teammates flew to Boston for the Ryder Cup. The American team had lost the cup in 1995 and 1997 by a total of two points, and the team was eager to win it back. As the players warmed up on Friday, September 24, none of them knew that they were about to take part in one of the greatest golf matches in history.

❝I always feel pressure. If you don't feel nervous, that means you don't care about how you play.❞

—TIGER WOODS

Tiger's Ryder Cup didn't start well. He and Tom Lehman lost their first match to Sergio Garcia and Jesper Parnevik. Tiger and David Duval then lost to Lee Westwood and Darren Clarke. Tiger was 0–2, and the American team was falling behind.

On Saturday, Tiger teamed up with Steve Pate. The pairing won its first match but lost a second match. The European team had built a huge lead, 10–6, going into the final day. The situation looked very bad for the American team. Twelve singles matches remained on Sunday. The American team needed 8.5 out of 12 points to win the cup. To many fans, it seemed an impossible task.

In a press conference Saturday night, American coach Ben Crenshaw told reporters not to count his team out. "I'm a big believer in fate," he said. "I have a good feeling about this."

After a pep talk from Texas governor George W. Bush, the American team hit the course, knowing how difficult the challenge ahead would be. As Sunday's singles matches began, Crenshaw remained confident.

Early on, the American team gave Crenshaw good reason to remain confident. Tom Lehman, Davis Love III, Phil Mickelson, and Hal Sutton had all won their matches, and suddenly the American team had pulled into a 10–10 tie. David Duval won his match to give the Americans the lead.

Tiger's match was next. Almost everyone in the crowd and the media had hoped Tiger would square off against his new rival, Sergio Garcia. But the coaches decided otherwise. His opponent was Andrew Coltart of Scotland. Tiger easily won the match, 3 and 2, increasing the American lead.

The American team didn't let up, and when Justin Leonard sank a seemingly impossible forty-five-foot putt, it was over. The Americans had completed an amazing comeback win. Players, coaches, and fans rushed onto the course to celebrate the win in a scene rarely seen in golf. "I never stopped believing," Crenshaw said. "I'm stunned. This is so indescribable."

Tiger was exhausted. He'd had a summer of incredible success. Already 1999 had been one of the best seasons any golfer had enjoyed in years. Tiger rewarded himself by taking some time off. He didn't play again for a month.

When Tiger returned to golf in late October, he was recharged and ready to pick up where he had left off. He planned to play in four more PGA Tour events before the end of the year. He hoped he would be able to add another win or maybe even two to his already great season.

Chapter Nine

Personal Grand Slam

Tiger returned to golf for the Disney Classic, held only a few miles from his Orlando home. He'd gone almost two months since winning the NEC Invitational, his last regular PGA Tour event, and almost one month since he and the American team had made their incredible comeback at the Ryder Cup.

Tiger built a big lead in the Disney Classic, shooting an impressive 66 in each of the first three rounds. Despite a disappointing score of 73 in the event's final round, Tiger held on to beat Ernie Els by a single stroke. It was his sixth win of the year. Nobody had won six events in a year since 1980. "I'd like to get seven, and then eight would be nice," Tiger said.

Tiger was on top of the golf world, but he couldn't enjoy it that week. On October 25, just one day after Tiger's win at the Disney Classic, friend and fellow golfer Payne Stewart was killed in an airplane crash.

After attending Stewart's funeral, Tiger went to Houston for the TOUR Championship. When he showed up for his round the next day, he looked at the list of tee times. The spot below his name was blank. It had been Stewart's spot. "I'm walking down the fairway and occasionally I get a few flashes in my head of Payne and some of the memories I have," Tiger said. "Everyone is going through that. It is just a matter of dealing with it and coming to . . . understand that he is in a better place right now."

Stewart had been a popular figure on the PGA Tour, famous for wearing pants called knickers. Many of the golfers at the TOUR Championship wore knickers to honor their fallen friend, but Tiger wasn't one of them. Tiger paid tribute to Payne Stewart in his own way—by winning. After beating second-place Davis Love III by four strokes, Tiger held his trophy high in the air and honored his friend. Because of the tragedy, many fans failed to notice that Tiger had won his seventh event of the year and his third in a row.

A week later, the focus returned to golf. The WGC–American Express Championship was the last big-money event of the year. The winner would take home $1 million. Tiger entered the final round trailing Miguel Angel Jimenez and Chris Perry by one stroke, but he quickly took over, building a two-stroke lead.

On the par-five 17th hole, Tiger played his first two shots carefully. Then he hit a nine-iron shot past the hole. The ball spun backward, toward the hole. It kept rolling back, sailing past the pin and dropping into a pond on the near side of the green. The hole was a disaster, a triple bogey. Suddenly the lead Tiger had worked all day to build was gone.

Tiger made par on the 18th hole and waited for Jimenez, who needed only a par to win the tournament and end Tiger's winning streak. But Jimenez bogeyed the hole to set up a playoff. Once Tiger had the momentum back, he wasn't about to let it go. He seemed to thrive in the pressure of the playoffs. He won the playoff and claimed his eighth win of the season. Even more amazing was that Tiger had won four PGA Tour events in a row, something no one had done in forty-six years.

---

66 *Nobody can touch this guy now at the moment. He's gone to another level that I don't think the rest of us can really find right now.* 99

—ERNIE ELS

Still, Tiger's amazing 1999 season wasn't over. He had one more event to play, the World Cup, which he won. It wasn't a PGA Tour event and didn't count toward his streak, but it was a fitting way to end the greatest season of golf in almost half a century. Again Tiger was named Player of the Year.

Tiger turned twenty-four at the end of the year. He was young and healthy, but the same couldn't be said of his father. Earl had already undergone three heart operations. He had prostate cancer. Tiger worried about his sick father, but he was also angry. Earl continued to smoke, drink, and eat badly. While the two remained close and Earl continued to help Tiger manage his career, Tiger realized it was time to start separating himself from his father. He needed to stand alone as the man in charge of his career. In 2000, Tiger took control on and off the course. As great as 1999 had been, Tiger wanted to have an even better 2000.

The first PGA Tour event of 2000 was the Mercedes Championships in Hawaii. Tiger's quest for a fifth-straight win wouldn't be easy. He and Ernie Els entered the final round in a back-and-forth fight for the lead. The golfers were tied going to the 18th hole, a monster 663-yard par five.

Both golfers smashed huge tee shots. Tiger then hit a three-wood shot to within fifteen feet of the hole. The crowd erupted as the shot came to a stop. Els answered Tiger's shot by striking a two-iron shot ten feet away from the pin. Again the crowd cheered. Both men made their putts, posting eagles on the hole and setting up a playoff.

The playoff started on the same hole, the 18th. This time, Tiger made a six-foot birdie putt to extend the match. On the second playoff hole, both golfers were looking at long putts for the win, Tiger from forty feet, Els from thirty-five. Tiger shot first. Almost in slow motion, he stepped sideways as he watched the ball roll to the hole and drop. He pumped his fist as the crowd cheered once more. Els still had a chance to tie, but his putt came up a foot short. Tiger had won again, starting 2000 where he'd left off in 1999. His winning streak was up to five.

"He's a legend in the making," Els said. "He's twenty-four. He's probably going to be bigger than Elvis."

TIGER'S CADDIES

Like any professional golfer, Tiger needs the help of a good caddie when choosing his shots. A caddie carries a golfer's bag and helps the golfer make decisions about how to play each shot.

Tiger's first caddie on the PGA Tour was Mike "Fluff" Cowan. Tiger and Cowan worked together for two and a half years before Tiger decided to make a change.

In 1999 Tiger asked Steve Williams to be his caddie. Williams had previously worked for Greg Norman and Ray Floyd. Working for Tiger has made Williams the most famous caddie in golf. He has made headlines several times for run-ins with photographers. He once kicked a camera after a photographer snapped a picture of Tiger while he was in the middle of an important shot.

The last player to win six straight PGA Tour events had been Ben Hogan in 1948. Tiger had a chance to match Hogan's accomplishment at the Pebble Beach National Pro-Am in California. Tiger played well in the first round, shooting a 68, but his score of 73 in the second dropped him way off the pace. After shooting a 68 in the third round, Tiger trailed leader Matt Gogel by five. His hopes for six wins in a row looked slim.

❝I've played enough with Tiger to see the way he plays. He's incredibly talented, yet he doesn't beat himself. When he takes a bad shot, he recovers. When he hits a good shot, he takes advantage of it.❞

—TOM LEHMAN

Those slim chances seemed to all but disappear as Gogel took a commanding seven-stroke lead with only seven holes to play. Tiger had made many great comebacks in his career, but making up seven strokes in seven holes seemed too much to ask of even the world's greatest golfer.

Suddenly the pressure got to Gogel, who began missing shots that he'd made all tournament long. Tiger took advantage. By the 15th hole, Tiger had cut Gogel's lead to just four strokes.

It was time for Tiger to make his move. His tee shot on the par-four hole set up a 97-yard pitch shot to the green. He appeared to be in good shape to make a birdie. Tiger grabbed his pitching wedge and stroked the ball several feet to the right of the hole. The ball spun downhill, toward the pin, and fell into the cup for a remarkable eagle. Gogel's lead had been sliced to two strokes. Tiger turned to one of the television cameras, smiled, and said, "I'm back in it!"

Tiger didn't let up. His pitch on the 16th hole landed three feet from the hole, and he had another birdie. He made another birdie on the last hole to take the lead, then waited for Gogel to finish his round. His final round score was 64.

"I figured I needed to birdie the last four holes," Tiger said. "I didn't do that, but I still played it four-under."

Gogel had to make a ten-foot birdie putt on the 18th hole to send the tournament into a playoff, but he missed it. It was over. Tiger had completed one of the biggest comebacks in PGA Tour history and had tied Ben Hogan's mark of six straight wins. He was more than halfway to breaking Byron Nelson's mark of eleven straight wins, a record most golf experts say can't be broken.

Tiger's bid to challenge Nelson's record ended at the Buick Invitational, which he had won the year before. This time around, Tiger's drives were wild. He missed fairway after fairway, and the rest of his game couldn't save him as he finished second. The streak was over, but Tiger remained by far the best golfer in the world.

With the streak finally behind him, Tiger had a chance to look ahead. The greatest, most difficult goal for many golfers is to win all four majors in the course of a career—a personal "Grand Slam." Only four golfers had accomplished this feat: Jack Nicklaus, Gary Player, Ben Hogan, and Gene Sarazen. (In a true Grand Slam, a player would win all four majors in the same year.)

 Tiger's official fan club is called Club Tiger. Fans can sign up through Tiger's official website, www.tigerwoods.com.

Tiger already had two majors under his belt. A personal Grand Slam would be nice, but Tiger wanted even more to hold all four titles at once. He already held the PGA Championship title from 1999. He needed to win the next three majors (the Masters, the British Open, and the U.S. Open) in 2000. Holding all four titles would be an almost unthinkable accomplishment, one that even the great Jack Nicklaus had never achieved.

After a poor finish at the Nissan Open and a second-place finish at the WGC–Accenture Match Play event, Tiger began his preparations for the Masters. He had two tournaments before heading to Augusta. He won the first, the Bay Hill Invitational, and finished second at The Players Championship.

Tiger arrived in Augusta in early April, confident and ready to play. He had spent weeks preparing, and Augusta was one of his favorite golf courses. But all his hard work meant nothing on the first day when Tiger shot a 75, dropping him well behind the leaders. He followed with a 72 on Friday, and his hopes of winning were all but gone. He came back in the final two rounds with good scores of 68 and 69, but he couldn't overcome his first two rounds, finishing fifth. If Tiger wanted to hold all four major titles at once, he would have to start over.

 In 2000 Tiger became the first athlete to be named *Sports Illustrated* Sportsman of the Year more than once.

After winning the Memorial Tournament, Tiger entered the next major, the U.S. Open. Many golf experts thought the U.S. Open would be the toughest major for Tiger to win because it didn't give a big advantage to golfers who hit long drives. Tiger was determined, though, and he wasn't going to give another major away on the first day. He shot a six-under round of 65 to take the lead. Tiger extended his lead to six strokes after two rounds and ten strokes entering the final round.

Tiger continued to dominate the field like no golfer had ever done in a major. Even his twelve-stroke win at the 1997 Masters couldn't match what he was doing at the U.S. Open. In his final twenty-six holes, he never scored worse than par. By the time it was over, Tiger had won the tournament by a jaw-dropping fifteen strokes, the largest-ever margin of victory in a major tournament. He also became the first player in U.S. Open history to shoot more than nine strokes under par.

"Records are great, but you don't really pay attention to that," Tiger said. "The only thing I know is I got the trophy sitting right next to me. To perform the way I did, and on one of the greatest venues in golf, it doesn't get much better than that."

With his U.S. Open title, the British Open remained the only major Tiger hadn't won. He got his chance a month later, and he didn't let it slip away. Again he dominated the tournament, much as he had the Masters in 1997 and the U.S. Open only a few weeks earlier. All four of Tiger's rounds were in the 60s, and he made only three bogeys in the tournament.

David Duval challenged Tiger for a while, trailing by only three strokes at one point, but he couldn't keep up down the stretch as Tiger scored an eight-stroke victory. It was Tiger's second major victory in a row. More important, it was the final piece of his personal Grand Slam. At age twenty-four, he was the youngest of the five players ever to win all four majors.

Despite the way Tiger had dominated two majors in a row, he wasn't completely happy with his game. When he was asked after the British Open if he was playing his best golf, he answered, "No, no, no, no. Definitely not."

Greatness wasn't enough. Tiger expected more of himself.

Chapter | Ten

Building a Legend

In August 2000, Tiger entered the PGA Championship looking to win a third-straight major. After his runaway wins at the U.S. Open and the British Open, Tiger was a heavy favorite to defend his title.

Tiger put himself in a comfortable position early, shooting rounds of 66 and 67 to open the tournament. But a third-round score of 70 allowed Bob May to catch up and set up a fantastic final round. Both golfers made some amazing shots in the final nine holes, including May's eighteen-foot birdie putt on the final hole. May's putt left Tiger with a bending six footer that he had to make to force a three-hole playoff. Tiger's putt caught the left edge of the hole and dropped in for the birdie.

Tiger took a one-stroke lead on the first playoff hole by sinking a twenty-five-foot birdie putt. Both players scored par on the second hole, meaning Tiger needed only to tie May on the third hole for the win. Tiger's tee shot sailed left and hit a tree, bouncing onto a cart path. His second shot landed in the rough. He then hit into a sand trap. But Tiger saved himself by hitting out of the sand, landing the ball only two feet from the hole. The easy putt saved par. Tiger could only wait as May lined up a long birdie try. May's putt missed. The playoff was over. Tiger had won his third major in a row, becoming the first golfer since Ben Hogan in 1953 to win three majors in the same year.

Tiger's summer of 2000 had been possibly the greatest stretch of golf anyone had ever played. He finished the year strongly, winning his next two events and never finishing outside the top five. By the year's end, he had played in twenty events, winning nine of them and finishing second four times. He finished in the top ten in seventeen of the twenty events he played, an amazing statistic in a sport where consistency is hard for even the greatest players. As good as Tiger's 1999 season had been, his 2000 season was unlike anything most golf fans had ever seen.

In 2001, Tiger published a book titled *Tiger Woods: How I Play Golf.* In the book, he gives readers tips and strategies on how to improve their golf games.

Tiger entered 2001 with one goal in mind. He needed only to win the Masters to hold all four major titles at one time, a feat no one had ever accomplished. Tiger still looked at his list of Jack Nicklaus's achievements, and this wasn't on the list. This was something that could set Tiger Woods apart from Nicklaus forever.

Tiger finished no better than fourth in the season's first five events, but he began to warm up at the Bay Hill Invitational, just a few weeks before the Masters. Tiger won that event, then won again at The Players Championship, sending him to Augusta with the momentum he wanted.

The scene at the Masters was even wilder and more crowded than usual. Fans and reporters swarmed Augusta, wanting to see Tiger's bid for what was being called a Tiger Slam. Some people argued that to complete a true Grand Slam, a player would have to win all four majors in the same year, but few people cared about that detail. They were there hoping to see Tiger make golf history once again. People lined up eight hours before Tiger was scheduled to tee off, eager to see him begin his charge.

Tiger didn't have a great first round, opening with a bogey on the first hole. He struggled with his putting and had to fight to a day-one score of 70, two strokes under par. His 66 in the second round put him right back among the leaders, though, and after a 68 on Saturday, he took the lead when he birdied three holes in a row. He carried the lead into the final day, but David Duval and Phil Mickelson were challenging.

The three golfers remained close throughout most of Sunday's final round. All three played well, but no one could distance himself from the others. Tiger finally had a chance on the 11th hole. He had a dangerous shot, with a lake to his left, rough to his right, and a tough uphill green straight ahead. Tiger pulled out his eight iron and ripped a near-perfect shot. The crowd roared as the ball rolled past the edge of the cup, giving Tiger a tap in for a birdie and the lead.

On the 15th hole, Tiger had a chance to build his lead to two strokes, but he missed a three-foot birdie putt. On the final hole, Tiger had an eighteen-foot putt for a birdie and the championship. He hit it just to the right of the hole, then watched it curve back and drop in. Tiger quickly took off his hat and held it over his face to hide tears of joy. He had won four majors in a row and five of the past six. It seemed that nothing could stop Tiger. "I've never had that feeling before," he said afterward.

Tiger struggled that summer and was unable to win another major in 2001, with finishes of twelfth, twenty-fifth, and twenty-ninth. But his season was a disappointment only because of the nearly impossible expectations he had created for himself. He finished the year with five wins in nineteen events, a mark any other golfer on the PGA Tour would have been thrilled to own. But Tiger wasn't any other golfer. He was Tiger Woods, and he wasn't happy with anything less than first.

In 2004 Tiger played in the Desert Classic at Dubai in the United Arab Emirates. While he was there, he hit golf balls off the top of the Burj Al Arab, the tallest hotel in the world at more than 1,000 feet.

In 2002 Tiger was determined to return to form in the majors. In April, he again went to Augusta to defend his title and win a third green jacket. Only Nicklaus and Nick Faldo had ever won the tournament in back-to-back years.

Tiger entered the final round tied with Retief Goosen but quickly built a two-stroke lead as Goosen struggled. He extended his lead to four strokes on the back nine, forcing his challengers to take risks that rarely succeeded. Tiger cruised to a twelve-under score of 276 and the victory. At age twenty-six, Tiger already had seven major wins, but he still stood eleven behind Nicklaus's lifetime record of eighteen.

Next up was the U.S. Open championship. Tiger jumped out to a quick lead with a three-under score of 67 on the first day. After rounds of 68 and 70, Tiger held a four-stroke lead over Sergio Garcia entering Sunday's round.

Early on Sunday, Tiger's play gave Garcia reason to believe he could come back. Tiger struggled with his putting on the first two holes, scoring a pair of bogeys and letting Garcia cut the lead in half. But Tiger focused himself and began playing well again. Any hopes Garcia had of coming back on Tiger were squashed on the 13th hole. Tiger smashed a two iron more than 260 yards, setting up a birdie that put him back in control. Despite struggling on the final hole, Tiger held on for a three-stroke win over the surging Phil Mickelson.

With wins in the first two 2002 majors, golf fans quickly started talking about a true Grand Slam. But Tiger's hopes of accomplishing that feat disappeared at the British Open, where he finished a disappointing twenty-eighth. He finished second in the final major of the year, the PGA Championship. He won two more tournaments in 2002, the Buick Open and the American Express Championship, giving him a total of five wins in eighteen events.

Although Tiger wanted to win every week, he was able to see that others winning was good for the game. "A lot of young kids are starting to win, the next generation of players, as well as some older players are winning that are surprises," he said in late 2002. "It's great to see that our tour is healthy, with that many good players out here."

While Tiger remained the top-ranked golfer on the PGA Tour, many of his fans wondered if he would ever return to his dominance of 2000. In 2003, he failed to win a major and was well out of contention in all but the British Open, where he finished fourth. Despite his disappointing performances in the 2003 majors, Tiger still managed to win five of the eighteen events he played, including an impressive nineteen-under-par win in the Bay Hill Invitational in March.

A DIFFERENT KIND OF TRAINING

Tiger has said that if he hadn't taken up golf, he might have followed in his father's footsteps and joined the military. In 2004 he spent two days training with the U.S. Army Special Operations Command at Fort Bragg, North Carolina. After his visit, he donated $50,000 to the Special Operations Warrior Foundation, a charity fund.

Still, Tiger wasn't happy with his season. He had spent his entire life improving; for the first time, he was having a difficult time matching his own achievements. Tiger was a victim of his own success. Simply being the best golfer in the world wasn't enough. People expected him to dominate the competition, to win every week, to never miss a putt or slice a drive. Even Tiger Woods couldn't live up to those expectations.

Epilogue

On and Off the Course

Tiger's life has changed drastically since he joined the PGA Tour. He used to feel pressure to prove himself every week, to show that he belonged. Today he knows he belongs. No matter what happens on the course, he has earned his place in golf history.

Tiger's life has changed in other ways as well. He no longer works with his longtime coach, Butch Harmon. He has continued to refine his golf swing, though, with the help of a friend, Hank Haney.

In late 2003 after the President's Cup in South Africa, Tiger and his girlfriend, Elin Nordegren, went for a sunset walk. During that walk, Tiger asked her to marry him. She said yes.

The couple finally married on October 5, 2004, at a resort on the Caribbean island of Barbados. After the wedding, the twenty-eight-year-old Tiger and his twenty-four-year-old bride boarded a yacht named *Privacy* to begin a long honeymoon.

Some golf experts have questioned whether Tiger's relationship with Elin has affected his golf game. After winning five or more tournaments in every year from 1998 through 2003, Tiger didn't win a single PGA Tour stroke-play event in 2004. In the Masters, he finished twenty-second, well out of contention. He continued to struggle at the U.S. Open, finishing seventeenth, fourteen strokes behind winner Retief Goosen. He did a little better at the British Open but still finished ninth. Finally, he struggled at the PGA Championship and, early on, was in danger of not even making the cut. He did end up making the cut but finished twenty-fourth. During his struggles in 2004, Tiger lost his number one ranking to Vijay Singh.

Tiger entered 2005 facing more pressure than even he was used to. People wanted to know why he'd struggled in 2004. They wondered if the old Tiger was gone forever. After finishing third in the season's first event, the Mercedes Championships, Tiger traveled to San Diego, California, for the Buick Invitational. He played well early. By the time fog forced him to suspend his round on Saturday, he was tied with Tom Lehman for the lead.

On Sunday Tiger woke up early to finish his third round. But he couldn't find his swing. He bogeyed his first three holes. He added another bogey on the final hole of the round and trailed Lehman by two strokes entering the final round. The week before, bad putting had cost Tiger a chance to win. This time, he knew putting would be the key to victory. While his swing wasn't the best in the final round, Tiger's putting was back in form. He hit putt after putt and kept the pressure on Lehman, cutting into his lead and then taking over first place. Finally, on the last hole, Tiger sank an eighteen-foot putt to complete the comeback.

"The start I kind of got off to this morning, it wasn't very good, but I hung in there," Tiger said after the win. "It's hard to believe it's been that long to win on our Tour, but it feels great."

A few weeks later, at the Doral Open Tiger set a tournament record by shooting twenty-four under par. He beat Phil Mickelson by one shot to win the event and reclaim his number one ranking.

Tiger's many fans hoped that his comeback win was a sign of things to come. And when Tiger won the 2005 Masters in a sudden-death playoff against Chris DiMarco, his return to the top was confirmed. No one can predict the course of his career, but a few things seem certain—Tiger has many years ahead of him on the PGA Tour, and he'll likely set at least a few more records before he's through.

PERSONAL STATISTICS

Name:

Eldrick Woods

Nicknames:

Tiger

Born:

December 30, 1975

Height:

6'2"

Weight:

180 lbs.

Residence:

Orlando, Florida

CAREER PGA TOUR STATISTICS

Year	Events	Wins	Top-5	Top-10	Earnings	Avg. Drive	Avg. Round
1992	1	0	0	0	$0	263.3	73.5
1993	3	0	0	0	$0	272.3	75.1
1994	3	0	0	0	$0	277.3	75.1
1995	4	0	0	0	$0	298.5	69.4
1996	11	2	5	5	$790,594	302.8	69.8
1997	21	4	7	9	$2,066,833	294.8	70.1
1998	20	1	8	13	$1,841,117	296.3	69.6
1999	21	8	13	16	$6,616,585	293.1	68.2
2000	20	9	17	17	$9,188,321	298.0	68.2
2001	19	5	8	9	$5,687,777	297.6	68.9
2002	18	5	11	13	$6,912,625	293.3	69.0
2003	18	5	11	12	$6,783,413	299.5	69.4
2004	19	1	9	14	$5,365,472	301.9	69.7

GLOSSARY

amateur: an athlete who is not paid for competing in a sport

approach shot: a shot designed to play the ball onto the green and to set up a putt

chip: a shot from near the green that lofts the ball to roll on the green

cut: the point at which, after a tournament's early rounds, the golfers with the worst scores are eliminated from the competition; golfers who "make the cut" continue playing

driver: the golf club that gives a golfer the farthest-possible distance on a shot

economics: the study of money and how to manage it

fairway: the short-cut grass between the tee and the green

gallery: the crowd gathered to watch a golf event

green: the very short-cut grass surrounding the pin

Green Beret: a soldier in the U.S. Army's special forces

iron: a club with a narrow, angled club face used for short drives, approach shots, and chips

knickers: loose-fitting, short pants

match: a head-to-head battle between two golfers; in match play, golfers compete to win the most holes

pitch shot: a shot from near the green that is mostly in the air, then rolls a short distance to the green

professional: an athlete who makes a living by competing in a sport

rookie: a first-year professional

rough: the thick grass outside the fairway

wood: a golf club with a long shaft and a large club head used for long drives and tee shots

SOURCES

1   Bill Gutman, *Tiger Woods: Golf's Shining Young Star* (Brookfield, CT: Millbrook Press, 1998), 41.

2   Ron Sirak, "Woods Wins in Record Fashion," *Golfweb.com,* April 13, 1997, http://services.golfweb.com/ga97/pga/0402/f.html (November 30, 2004).

5   Gutman, *Tiger Woods,* 8.

9   John Strege, *Tiger: A Biography of Tiger Woods* (New York: Broadway Books, 1998), 16.

11 Ibid., 30.

14 Ibid., 37.

14 Gutman, *Tiger Woods,* 18.

15 Strege, *Tiger,* 48–49.

16 Ibid., 41.

17 Glenn Stout, ed., *Chasing Tiger: The Tiger Woods Reader* (Cambridge, MA: Da Capo Press, 2002), 12.

18 Gutman, *Tiger Woods,* 18.

24 Strege, *Tiger,* 50.

25 Blaine Newnham, "Four! Tiger Stalking Another Title at NEC Invitational," *tigertales.com,* August 22, 2002, http://www.tigertales.com/1998/2002/tiger/four0822.html (November 30, 2004).

27 Tim Rosaforte, "The Comeback Kid," *SI.com,* September 5, 1994, http://sportsillustrated.cnn.com/features/1996/sportsman/archive/940905.html (Novemeber 30, 2004).

29 Strege, *Tiger,* 75.

30 Tim Rosaforte, "The Comeback Kid," *SI.com,* September 5, 1994, http://sportsillustrated.cnn.com/features/1996/sportsman/archive/940905.html (Novemeber 30, 2004).

30 Ibid.

30 Strege, *Tiger,* 77.

33 Ibid., 81–82.

36 ASAP Sports, "Tiger Woods: Tries to Emulate Nicklaus' Consistency," *golfserv.com,* October 29, 2002, http://www.golfserv.com/gdc/news/article.asp?id=8638 (November 30, 2004).

40 "Woods Repeats as U.S. Amateur Champion," *washingtonpost.com,* August 28, 1995, http://www.washingtonpost.com/wp-srv/sports/longterm/memories/1995/95golf3.htm (November 30, 2004).

40 Strege, *Tiger,* 120.

41 Rob Mueller, "Woods Called 'Most Fundamentally Sound Golfer'," *SI.com,* 2000, http://sportsillustrated.cnn.com/augusta/news/0410/nick.html (March 8, 2005).

45 Strege, *Tiger,* 177.

45 James Diaz, "Roaring Ahead," *SI.com,* September 2, 1996, http://sportsillustrated.cnn.com/features/1996/sportsman/archive/960902.html (November 30, 2004).

46 Ibid.

47 Gutman, *Tiger Woods,* 25.

49 Leigh Monteville, "On the Job Training in Milwaukee, the Professional Debut of Amateur Champ Tiger Woods Was a Qualified Success," *Golfweb.com,* n.d., http://services.golfweb.com/si/1996/0901/tiger.html (November 30, 2004).

51 Gutman, *Tiger Woods,* 34.

52 Gary Smith, "The Chosen One," *SI.com,* n.d., http://sportsillustrated.cnn.com/features/1996/sportsman/1996.html (November 30, 2004).

57 Gary Van Sickle, "JACKPOT!" *SI.com,* October 14, 1996, http://sportsillustrated.cnn.com/features/1996/sportsman/archive/961014.html (November 30, 2004).

57 Ibid.

58 Gutman, *Tiger Woods,* 35.

60 Ibid., 37.

61 Tim Rosaforte, *Raising The Bar: The Championship Years of Tiger Woods* (New York: St. Martin's Press, 2000), 99.

62 Bob Verdi, "Warm and Fuzzy," *GolfDigest.com,* April 13, 2001, http://www.golfdigest.com/features/index.ssf?/features/warm_and_25we3elc.html (March 1, 2005).

63 Denne H. Freeman, "Just Wants to Talk about Woods," *tigertales.com,* n.d., http://www.tigertales.com/tiger/kite041497.html (November 30, 2004).

68 "Woods Completes Record Run at Open," *espn.com,* June 19, 2000, http://espn.go.com/golfonline/usopen_m00/s/2000/0618/591961.html (November 30, 2004).

69 Bob Harig, "Harig: Woods Thinks Positive After Close Call," *espn.com,* n.d., http://espn.go.com/golfonline/premium/tours/bobharig/1999/990620/00001510.html (November 30, 2004).

71 Rosaforte, *Raising the Bar,* 155.

73 "Tiger Weathers El Niño," *SI.com,* August 16, 1999, http://sportsillustrated.cnn.com/golf/1999/pga_championship/news/1999/08/15/pga_sunday/index.html (November 30, 2004).

73 "Tiger On Playing Under Pressure," *tigerwoods.com,* September 10, 2003, http://www.tigerwoods.com/news/fullstory.sps?iNewsid=115751&itype=6264&iCategoryID=506 (November 30, 2004).

74 "1999 Ryder Cup: U.S. 14 1/2, Europe 13 1/2," *golfserv.com,* n.d., http://www.golfserv.com/rydercup/history/year.asp?year=1999 (November 30, 2004).

75 Ibid.

76 Rosaforte, *Raising the Bar,* 164.

77 "Tour Players Struggle with Stewart's Death," *usatoday.com,* October 26, 1999, http://www.usatoday.com/sports/golf/stewart/stewfs02.htm (November 30, 2004).

78 Rosaforte, *Raising the Bar,* 169.

80 "Tiger Woods Wins Fifth Consecutive PGA Golf Tournament – Mercedes Championship," *Looksmart.com,* January 24, 2000, http://articles.findarticles.com/p/articles/mi_m1355/is_7_97/ai_59164778 (November 30, 2004).

81 Rosaforte, *Raising the Bar,* 170.

82 "Huge Comeback Gives Woods Sixth Straight Win," *espn.com,* February 8, 2000, http://espn.go.com/golfonline/tours/pga/2000/20000207/00004230.html (November 30, 2004).

82 Ibid.

85 "Woods Completes Record Run at Open," *espn.com,* June 19, 2000, http://espn.go.com/golfonline/usopen_m00/s/2000/0618/591961.html (November 30, 2004).

86 "Woods Just Grand with British Win," *espn.com,* July 24, 2000, http://espn.go.com/golfonline/britishopen00/s/2000/0723/647995.html (November 30, 2004).

90 "Woods Grabs Piece of History at Augusta," *espn.com,* April 20, 2001, http://espn.go.com/golfonline/masters01/s/2001/0408/1169595.html (November 30, 2004).

92 ASAP Sports, "Talking With . . . Tiger Woods," *detnews.com,* December 4, 2002, http://www.detnews.com/2002/golf/0212/06/b04-26816.htm (January 25, 2005).

96 "Tiger Woods Press Conference," *tigerwoods.com,* January 24, 2005, http://www.tigerwoods.com/news/fullstory.sps?inewsid=144589&iType=6245 (January 25, 2005).

BIBLIOGRAPHY

Feinstein, John. *The First Coming: Tiger Woods: Master or Martyr?* New York: Ballantine, 1998.

Gutman, Bill. *Tiger Woods: Golf's Shining Young Star.* Brookfield, CT: Millbrook Press, 1998.

Rosaforte, Tim. *Raising the Bar: The Championship Years of Tiger Woods.* New York: St. Martin's Press, 2000.

Sirimarco, Elizabeth. *Tiger Woods.* Mankato, MN: Capstone Books, 2001.

Stewart, Mark. *Tiger Woods: Driving Force.* New York: Children's Press, 1998.

Stout, Glenn, ed. *Chasing Tiger: The Tiger Woods Reader.* Cambridge, MA: Da Capo Press, 2002.

Strege, John. *Tiger: A Biography of Tiger Woods.* New York: Broadway Books, 1998.

Woods, Earl. *Training a Tiger: A Father's Guide to Raising a Winner in Both Golf and Life.* New York: HarperCollins, 1997.

Woods, Tiger. *How I Play Golf.* New York: Warner Books, 2001.

WEBSITES

Official Website for Tiger Woods

http://tigerwoods.com

Tiger's official site includes news updates, statistics, quotations, games, and even golfing tips from Tiger.

The PGA Tour's Official Website

http://www.pgatour.com

The official site of the PGA Tour includes player biographies, statistics, live scoring, results, and feature articles.

ESPN.com Golf

http://sports.espn.go.com/golf/index

ESPN.com's golf site features news about past and upcoming golf events, player biographies, statistics, leaderboards, and feature articles.

SI.com—Golf

http://sportsillustrated.cnn.com/golf/

Sports Illustrated's website has a section devoted to golf with plenty of articles and information on the top players.

INDEX

106